GIFTED

AND

EMPOWERED

SECRETS TO UNLOCK AND USE YOUR UNIQUE BRILLIANCE CONFIDENTLY

CAROLE D. MONTEIRO

All inquiries should be made to:
hello@caroledmonteiro.com

Book cover art by Getcovers.com

DISCLAIMER

The following viewpoints or advice in this book are those of Carole D. Monteiro. These views are based on her personal experience over the past forty-five years on the planet Earth, especially while living in the United Kingdom.

The intention of this book is to share her story and experience about discovering the untapped potential that is within us and what has worked for her through this journey.

All attempts have been made to verify the information provided by this publication. Neither the author nor the publisher assumes any responsibility for errors, omissions, or contrary interpretations of the subject matter herein.

This book is for entertainment purposes only. The views expressed are those of the author alone and should not be taken as expert instruction or commands. The reader is responsible for his or her future action. This book makes no guarantees of future success. However, by following the steps that are listed in this book, the odds of discovering and using your gifts to serve others have a much higher probability.

Neither the author nor the publisher assumes any responsibility or liability on behalf of the purchaser or reader of this publication.

The views expressed are based on the author's personal experiences within the corporate and non-profit world, education, and everyday life.

Table of Contents

ACKNOWLEDGMENTS

Thank you GOD for love, grace, strength, guidance and for the gifts entrusted to me.

Thank YOU, dear reader, for investing your time reading this book.

Thank you to my loving and amazing husband, "Manu". Without your constant support and motivation – and incredible patience – I would literally not be here and have a finished book today.

Thank you to my awesome sister, Sabrina, who has been my constant cheerleader and has seen 'a few' previous versions of this book. Your advice and support have been invaluable.

And of course, I could not forget "Mam". Thank you to my mom, who is a lifelong learner and always rises to challenges. She reminds me that 'everything you seek is within you' as she would so rightfully tell her grandchildren.

Thank you to my fabulous "Entrepreneur Sisters", Karen and Olivia, for keeping me accountable and inspiring me to commit to my goals and tick those boxes weekly. And thank you Anne, Katia, Inês and Maria for constantly cheering me on.

Thank you to my dear "Ladies Club" sister-friends Amanda, Liv, Michelle, Ruth and Tanya. Also Natasha and Natalie. Your laughter and consistent friendship over the years – in the great, the bad, and the ugly seasons – bring me joy and keep me going.

I dedicate this book to every woman I have had the privilege to help grow and gain more confidence to go after their dreams through starting a business, transitioning into a new career, changing their mindset on their circumstances, embracing motherhood at a later age, or finishing what they started.

You have all gone above and beyond chasing your dreams and I am proud to be a part of your journey.

And lastly, to my son, G., "can you believe that 'maman' (that's me!) wrote a book?" I can confidently say that every mother (secretly) wants her children to be proud of her. This book is my legacy to my awesome boy. I want him to remember me as someone who was in the business of making her dreams become a reality.

It is with a spirit of celebration that I add a big tick on my list of things to accomplish. It is done! With faith, truly the impossible becomes possible!

HOW EMPOWERED ARE YOU?

Are you ready to uncover how truly empowered you are and tap into your full potential to make a meaningful difference? Why not try this fun and enlightening quiz to delve into your present level of self-empowerment? It's a chance to see where you are at, get inspiration to transform your life and exercise your unique brilliance to make a profound impact on others. Step into the shoes of the exceptional woman you're destined to be and let your empowerment radiate brightly.

"HOW EMPOWERED ARE YOU?"

TAKE THE QUIZ BELOW TO FIND OUT:

Or go to: https://mindfulteabreak.involve.me/how-empowered-are-you
(Your full results will be available in Chapter 7).

PREFACE

The Journey Begins

When I first started on this journey of writing a book, it was somewhere around July 2017. It was great because I was working on a journey to share some of my observations, insight, and experience to hopefully help someone else see all the potential they have within them and all the possibilities in front of them. However, being a first-time writer, I slowly became discouraged, got busy with life and I started to forget about the book all together as I no longer made it a priority.

As I am writing this now, it is 2024. Seven years on, and the whole world has pretty much gone through a new normal after many changes. Do you agree that A LOT has gone on these last few years? Being based in the UK, we went through Brexit in January 2020. There have been market disruptions, a worldwide pandemic, conflicts, a looming recession, sky high inflation, job redundancies, AI...

So much has changed... And the truth is many people are still struggling to come to terms with whatever loss they've experienced.

Personally, before all these events occurred, I was pretty confident that I would use the time on my hand to fully work on this precious little project of writing this book, and I would be able to finish it this time around! I'd written my first two chapters during that time and felt so proud. Only that, then, I went through other changes. One of them was becoming pregnant. It was a sudden, happy, yet challenging time as I went through my first pregnancy at forty-two years old. A new chapter in my own life... So, after a break to focus on being a new mother, I started again at the end of 2021. Needless to say, it has been a journey, but one that I will always cherish and be thankful for!

With these challenges going on during my seven years of writing this book, it helped shape my experience better on how valuable one's gifts are, truly. Throughout the years, I have come to realise that we all have gifts and that without using those gifts, it is impossible to move forward in truly living a life of purpose. I have also discovered that when you live a life of purpose through your gifts, there is nothing that can stop you, and you, thereby, become a gift.

I chose to write my first book on gifts after listening to a webinar on how to write a book. In the workshop, we were asked to take a piece of paper, and the task was to write what our book was going to be about. I wrote these exact two sentences: “I would like to write about 'what's in your house,' basically recognising and using the skills, talents, and even experiences and mistakes that we have accumulated in life to become our greatest asset. Using everything we have experienced in life to re-write our story in a way that makes us successful in life". This is how I came about the topic of the book.

Subsequently, I chose and began to write this book because I believe that it needs to first start with me being open to discovering my own gifts. In this case, I was opened to discovering my writing gift, potentially, of which I realised that until I had completed this book, I wouldn’t know whether it is truly a gift of mine. So, I took on this challenge to start and finish the book, accepting what is and what may not be along the way.

But first… Who is this book for? This book is intended for, but not limited to, women who, like me, have been wondering about what the future holds. Women who believe there's more to life than just being a mother, a wife, single, retired or following a regular job. If you have a sense that there's something greater waiting for you, this book is for you. And if you don't fit into any of these categories, I welcome you with open arms as we embark on this empowering journey together. It's all about discovering your true identity beyond what others see.

You will see throughout the book that I use real-life stories to illustrate my points. I have purposely changed my friends' and acquaintances' names in order to protect their privacy.

Throughout the book I have included some biblical references, though it is not written solely for Christian women. It is for any woman who has faith in a brighter future and believes she has a role to play in this world. I encourage you to approach the content with an open mind. I believe you are capable of achieving amazing things, and this book will inspire and guide you towards the amazing possibilities that lie ahead.

In the process of writing this book, I faced numerous challenges, but the most significant one was grappling with the fear of inadequacy. I told myself a few times: "English is not my native language; who am I to publish a book, after all...?". However, I overcame this fear when I realised that my unique observations, insights, and ideas are valuable in their own right, knowing that they might differ from others, and that's okay. We all have distinct experiences and find ourselves in different situations, so it's natural for our perspectives to vary.

As I share this work with you, my aim is not to dictate what you should do, nor do I claim to have all the answers. Instead, I hope to spark something within you, to ignite a flame of curiosity and self-reflection. My wish is that you discover the immense power within yourself and find the courage to utilise your talents, gifts, and skills. When we share our inner gifts with others, we create a beautiful cycle of blessings – not just for ourselves but for those around us as well.

Let me make it clear; I am no expert claiming to have it all figured out. Rather, I am on a journey of self-discovery, just like you. And if someone like me can write this book, regardless of the time it took, then I am confident that you too can discover your gifts and talents.

It's time to shift our thinking, take a fresh perspective on what the world has to offer, and consider what we can offer in return. What blessings, talents, or gifts do you possess that can enrich the world and those around you?

I humbly continue on this journey, knowing that the content of this book has the potential to be as transformative for you as it has been for me. Let's embrace the greatness within us. Together, we can make a difference and create a brighter future for ourselves and those around us.

I am truly thankful for this opportunity to speak in writing what is in my heart. And before you dive into the content of the book, let me leave you with an inspiring quote.

This is from the poet Rumi: "As you start to walk out on the way, the way appears." This quote speaks to the power of taking action and trusting that the path will reveal itself as we move forward. It's easy to feel overwhelmed and unsure when facing a new challenge or journey but taking that first step is often the most important part.

Let us have faith in ourselves and in the journey ahead, even when it feels daunting. With belief and action, all things are possible, and the path will reveal itself as we walk it.

As you go on to reading the chapters ahead, I invite you to remember that the inspiration you seek is already within you. Take the time – as much as required – to listen to your inner voice, and trust in your own intuition and abilities. You may find that, often, we look for external sources of motivation and guidance when, in reality, the answers we seek are already present within ourselves.

Finally, my aspiration is that this book be a valuable companion in your quest to discover your gifts and fulfil your life's purpose. May it ignite a fire of inspiration within you, enabling you to embrace your distinct talents and pursue your passions with unwavering confidence and courage.

Chapter 1

Unwrapping Your Gift: Embrace the Power Within!

"The greatest tragedy in life is not death, but a life without a purpose." - Myles Munroe

What is a gift? Have you ever taken a moment to truly consider the question? You might have a specific notion in mind. Is it a talent, like a melodious voice or the ability to craft beautiful lyrics? Or is it a unique ability, such as an extraordinary talent for dancing? While these are certainly gifts, it's worth noting that the concept of a gift extends far beyond these examples.

So, what then, is a gift? To start simply, it's something in which we naturally excel, activities that require little effort yet bring immense joy, effortlessly unfolding into success. These are things that may not come as easily to others. Your gifts are your strengths, the tools you can use to achieve your aspirations and find satisfaction in life. Even though some gifts might need a bit of work to develop, they're usually things that come naturally to you.

Consider this – are you known for your innovative ideas? If you've been praised for this ability, then this is one of your unique gifts. But remember, there may be other gifts within you that you have yet to uncover.

It's important that you trust in yourself and recognise the potential you hold. You weren't born an empty vessel; there's something truly special and valuable within you, your gift. And until you acknowledge it, you might never realise your full potential.

It is essential then, to discover and nurture our gifts. After all, they could be the key to leading fulfilling and purposeful lives.

1. How are all Gifts Special and Unique?

You possess a unique set of gifts that distinguishes you from everyone else. These gifts can take many forms, some visible, some hidden, but all equally precious and deserving of recognition.

It's easy to fall into the trap of comparing yourself with others, isn't it? You may even feel as though your gifts are less significant. But that's a misperception. Each gift is unique and serves a specific purpose. No two individuals share the exact same combination of gifts. That's what makes you special and allows you to contribute distinctively to the world.

Have you considered that gifts can be tangible or intangible? Perhaps you're artistically talented, musically gifted, or athletically inclined. Or maybe your gifts are more abstract like kindness, compassion or empathy. Regardless of their form, all gifts are equally valuable and significant.

Isn't it wonderful that our gifts come naturally to us? We don't need to strain or struggle; they simply flow from us, bringing joy and fulfilment. Your gifts are what you excel at, often in areas that others might find challenging.

Notice how your gifts can connect you with others. When you use your gifts, you have the capacity to inspire and enrich the lives of those around you. It's an opportunity to share your unique abilities with the world and make a positive impact.

Let's take a moment to reflect on an example. Remember the dishes your mother, stepmother, or guardian used to prepare when you were a child? As an adult, you've tried other dishes, but none quite compares to those home-cooked meals, right? It's not just about the unique style or seasonings but also the unique touch that comes from them. This uniqueness can be seen as a gift.

Now, think about this in relation to your own gifts. Your gifts are bestowed upon you by your creator, meant to serve a specific purpose. Whether it's to inspire, help, protect, build, lead, spread joy, or give hope, your gift is unique and valuable.

Have you ever noticed how you can identify a singer just by their voice or singing style? That's because, even though many are gifted with the ability to sing, each artist brings their unique touch to their music.

So, are you hesitating to share your gifts because you fear the field is too crowded? Remember, your gift is unique and will be appreciated. Maybe not by everyone, but certainly by those who resonate with it.

I hope this helps you understand how your gifts make you who you are. They allow you to connect with others, make a positive impact, and find joy and fulfilment in life. So, will you embrace your gifts, recognise their value, and use them to make a difference in the world?

2. You are never a Mistake: Your Gift's Uniqueness begins with who you are

Have you ever felt less than perfect? Like, you ever looked in the mirror and wished you were someone else, someone "better"? I've been there, and I can tell you, it's a lonely place to be. Growing up, I felt that my small frame and lack of curves made me unattractive, less appealing than other girls. I constantly felt like I wasn't good enough, and these negative thoughts deeply affected my self-esteem.

But guess what? It was all a lie. I was deceiving myself. Over time, I came to understand that there were people who found my body type attractive and appreciated me for who I truly was, not just how I looked. This was a life-changing revelation for me: I am unique, and everything about me serves a purpose.

So, let me tell you this: You are not a mistake, worthless, or empty. Everything about you, from your appearance to your personality to your interests, has a purpose. You can only discover your unique gifts when you accept and love yourself for who you are.

Your strengths, talents, and passions are all clues to your unique gift. It takes work and strategies to discover them, but it's a journey worth taking.

That's why I wrote this book. I wanted to share the steps and knowledge you need to discover and utilise your unique gift. You have something special within you, and this book can help you unleash your full potential.

Remember this: You were never born empty. Your gift is waiting to be discovered, and it all begins with loving and accepting yourself for who you are.

The Bible says, "For you created my inmost being; you knit me together in my mother's womb. I praise you because I am fearfully and wonderfully made." (Psalm 139:13-14). This verse means every part of you was created for a purpose. Just like a skilled knitter creates a beautiful garment, God formed every part of you.

The word "fearful" here means to be in awe, and "wonderfully" means exceptionally or amazingly. So, my dear reader, this verse reminds you that you are a masterpiece!

As Pablo Picasso, the famous Spanish painter, said, **"You are a marvel. You are unique..."**. Your

Creator has blessed each of us with a special gift. He has chosen YOU for a specific purpose and given you unique and precious gifts.

These gifts come in all sorts of forms. Each gift is uniquely crafted to match your personality, talents, and purpose. It's like receiving a beautifully wrapped gift, made just for you.

George Lucas once said, "**Everybody has talent; it's just a matter of moving around until you've discovered what it is**". This talent is your gift. It's something special within you that you can offer to others.

Discovering your talent takes time and patience. Allow yourself to try new things, make mistakes, and remember that every experience is a stepping-stone on your path to self-discovery.

I encourage you to embrace your uniqueness. Your journey is yours alone and your talent is as unique and beautiful as you are.

Before you start doubting that you have any special talent, ask yourself this: Have you explored enough to discover your gift? Exploring isn't just about physically moving around your surroundings. It's about exploring your inner world and uncovering your unique strengths and abilities.

You may have doubts, especially when you compare yourself to others or when life gets tough. But always remember this: you have something remarkable within you, waiting to be discovered and used for good.

Are you ready to delve deeper into the journey of self-discovery? Fantastic! Stay tuned, because in the next chapter, we're going to uncover even more about this fascinating journey. Don't stop reading now – the best is yet to come!

3. Gift and Passion: Unveiling Your True Potential

Have you ever wondered if your passion could be your gift? This question takes centre stage, especially for us women, as we navigate our dreams and interests. Distinguishing between passion and gift is crucial in the quest to unlock our full potential. Though they may seem similar, these two concepts hold unique implications for our life journey. Ready to dive in and explore this together?

Passion is that spark of intense enthusiasm that lights up our hearts. Think about that one activity, hobby, or interest that sets your heart on fire. You might say, "I have a passion for books and dream of becoming an author." However, it's important to ask yourself if this passion is just a desire or if it's rooted in a latent talent waiting to bloom. Have you received compliments on your writing skills or been praised for your literary flair? If so, this could be more than just a passing passion; it could be an undiscovered gift waiting to be nurtured.

Consider this: "I'm passionate about becoming a doctor because I respect the societal admiration they receive." This statement shows a strong desire but doesn't necessarily point to a gift. The passion might be fuelled by external factors or societal expectations, not an innate talent for medicine. Remember, while passions can be intense and inspirational, they can also be fleeting. Some may persist due to our relentless desire, but that doesn't automatically make them our true gifts.

On the flip side, a gift is something inherent within us. It's not something we have to hunt for or strive to achieve; it's a natural ability or talent waiting to be discovered and honed. Each one of us has unique gifts that span various areas like saving, helping, protecting, building, leading, making a difference, bringing joy, shedding light, giving hope, and providing relief, among many others.

While passion is fuelled by desire, a gift serves a higher purpose – it fulfils a mission. It's meant to be shared with the world for others' benefit. Sometimes, our passions can lead us to our gifts. They can open doors and hint at our true talents. Yet, they can also lead us astray if we get fixated on something that doesn't mesh with our real strengths.

It's vital to uncover and embrace our God-given gifts and talents to unlock our true potential. Think of it as finding the key to our destiny's door. Our passion, though inspiring, shouldn't be confused with our gift without careful scrutiny. Our gift is our strength, and once we identify it, we can channel our passion towards using and perfecting that gift. The fusion of gift and passion sets the stage for excellence and fulfilment.

As women, we often find ourselves playing multiple roles – mothers, wives, single women, career professionals, or entrepreneurs. It's natural to yearn for more in life – to explore beyond our current situations and discover the extraordinary within ourselves. Embracing our gifts allows us to transcend societal expectations and embark on a journey of self-discovery and empowerment.

So, ladies, as you continue to explore your passions and interests, take a moment to reflect if they align with your gifts. While passions can ignite our spirits and inspire us, it is our gifts that truly define our strengths and purpose. Let your natural abilities guide you towards your purpose. Harness your strengths and talents, and let your passion stoke the fire within you as you step into a world of unlimited possibilities. Remember, you are destined for greatness, and your gifts are the key to unlocking your extraordinary potential. Embrace them, believe in them, and let them shape your path to a life of purpose, joy, and significance.

However, before we get too far, it's important to understand that there are two types of gifts: natural gifts and spiritual gifts. Let's delve into the differences between these.

4. Unveiling Natural Gifts

Have you ever thought about the unique gifts you possess? Let's delve into the intriguing world of Natural Gifts. They're those innate skills and abilities that are second nature to you. It's like you were born to do them. In some cases, you might need to take a course to refine them, but the core ability is just in you. Imagine that!

These natural gifts, they're not something you acquire; they're something you're born with and continue to discover as you age. Think about it, are you naturally good at singing, drawing, acting, or maybe dancing? Do you effortlessly play a musical instrument or excel at sports? Or perhaps, you're a natural at public speaking or making people laugh?

But wait, there's more to natural gifts than just talents. You could be naturally gifted at showing compassion, leading others, or memorising things. Maybe you're a fast reader, a good listener, or have a knack for counselling. Are you someone who picks up languages quickly or can speak in various accents flawlessly? Perhaps you're influential, a natural-born teacher, or have a warm and inviting smile.

Surprised to see "smiling" on this list? The discovery of your natural gifts can indeed be full of surprises. Yes, a warm, infectious smile is a genuine gift. Do people often comment on your smile? Consider the power it holds; it can brighten up someone's day, lift their spirits, and spread joy like magic.

Have you ever thought about how a simple act of kindness, a word of hope, or even just a warm smile can impact others? Let me share a personal experience. Some years back, I was feeling pretty low. I ended up on a train ride home, sitting across from an older man. As our eyes met, he gave me the gentlest and warmest of smiles. It felt divine, and I felt comforted, as if he was telling me everything would be okay. That smile changed not only my day – it changed my whole outlook on life.

So, don't downplay your gifts. They might seem small or insignificant to you, but they could be life-changing for others. Your inner gifts are unique and natural to you, while they might be things that others find challenging or struggle to learn.

Remember, your gifts are special. They can make a difference in someone's life. Embrace them, cherish them, and use them to bring joy, comfort, and positivity to the world around you. They're a beautiful part of who you are and could lead you towards a fulfilling and purposeful life. So, why not share your warm smile and your many other gifts? Embrace your uniqueness and let your light shine brightly!

Purpose of Natural Gifts

Have you ever thought about the purpose of your natural gifts? They are more than just personal attributes. They play an essential role in **bringing meaning and fulfilment to your life and the lives of those around you**. You see, we all have unique talents and skills, in areas such as creativity, problem-solving, communication, empathy, leadership, or organisation. Have you identified yours yet? Acknowledging and embracing your natural gift could unlock your true potential, allowing you to contribute to something larger than yourself.

Have you considered how you can use your natural gift to serve others? This could be through your profession, volunteering, or even personal relationships. Your gift holds the power to uplift and support those around you. Are you the one everyone turns to for advice? Your keen listening skills and wisdom could be a comfort to a friend in need. Do you have a knack for organisation? Your skills could help a non-profit or community group run more efficiently. The potential of your gift to bring joy, relief, and inspiration to others is immense – imagine the difference you could make!

And let's not forget the personal growth that comes with nurturing your natural gift. As you develop and explore your talent, you'll inevitably face challenges and opportunities for growth. Doesn't that sound exciting? It pushes you out of your comfort zone, inspires you to learn new things, and develop valuable skills. For instance, are you a fantastic public speaker who struggles with nerves? Embracing your gift could help you overcome your fears and become a more confident communicator. Each step you take in using your gift allows you to expand your abilities, gain new experiences, and become an even better version of yourself. Now, isn't that an exciting prospect?

Think about a time when someone complimented you on something you did effortlessly. Could this be one of your natural gifts? Write down your thoughts and experiences, and consider how you might nurture this gift further.

____

____

____

____

____

____

____

Just remember this. Your natural gift is of great importance in your life. It's a unique expression of who you are and what you have to offer the world. By acknowledging, embracing, and using your gift, you can make a difference in the lives of others, find personal fulfilment, and embark on a journey of continued growth and self-discovery. Embrace it with confidence, and watch as it transforms not just your life, but also the lives of those you touch.

5. Unveiling Spiritual Gifts

As we continue on this journey of self-discovery, let's dive into the subject of Spiritual Gifts. You may wonder, what exactly are these? Well, they are special abilities or qualities that reside within each of us. They are not tied to our birth or our genes. They are the unique form of empowerment that comes from developing a connection with a divine source, often referred to as God. These gifts are sacred, playing a significant role in enriching not just our own lives, but also those around us. To truly appreciate and make the most of these spiritual gifts, it's essential to value them and recognise the blessings they represent.

Now, you may or may not share my Christian faith, and that's okay. This isn’t about religion. To help you understand what spiritual gifts might look like, let's consider a few examples. Have you ever found yourself naturally uplifting those around you? Do you have a knack for offering a listening ear or imparting words of wisdom? That's the gift of encouragement. Or you might have the ability to empathise deeply with others, to connect with their feelings and experiences. This empathetic nature is another spiritual gift. Some of you might be gifted in teaching, simplifying complex ideas, and inspiring others to learn and grow. Perhaps your talent lies in creative expression, bringing beauty and inspiration into the world through art, music, or writing.

Leadership is another spiritual gift. You may naturally inspire and motivate others to reach their goals, with an ability to see the bigger picture and organise people and resources effectively. Some of you might possess the gift of discernment and the ability to offer wise counsel, helping others make informed decisions based on intuition and insight.

Do you find joy in helping others, in volunteering, caregiving, or just being there for someone in need? These acts of service and compassion are also spiritual gifts, bringing light and hope to those facing challenges.

These are just a few examples. There are many more, varying from person to person. Discovering your spiritual gifts can be an enlightening experience. Looking at certain verses in the Bible might give you insights into the specific spiritual gifts you possess.

For example, Romans 12:6-8 talks about prophesying, serving others, teaching, encouraging others, giving, leading, and showing kindness.

1 Corinthians 12:8-10 mentions wise advice, special knowledge, great faith, healing, miracles, prophesy, discernment of spirits, speaking in diverse languages (tongues), and interpreting unknown languages.

Ephesians 4:11 pointed out these gifts: apostle, prophet, evangelist, pastor, teacher.

And 1 Peter 4:10-11 stated these gifts: speaking, helping others.

The key is to recognise and embrace these unique gifts. They are integral to who you are and what you have to offer the world. So, are you ready to discover your spiritual gifts?

Purpose of Spiritual Gifts

Have you ever wondered about true purpose of your spiritual gifts? These are not mere talents to be hoarded or used for personal gain. Instead, they serve a higher purpose. Think of them as seeds planted within you, yearning to blossom and enrich the world around you.

Consider this: What if the purpose of your spiritual gifts is to **nurture connections and foster community**? The apostle Paul, in 1 Corinthians 12:4-6, reminds us that our spiritual gifts stem from the unified Trinity — God the Father, the Son, the Holy Spirit. His message highlights the diverse origins of these gifts, all coming from the same divine source. Could Paul's wisdom be an invitation for us to appreciate unity and collaboration, essential qualities rooted at the heart of spiritual gifts? Can you see how disunity might stunt the growth and influence of our community? Yet, by using our gifts, we can foster a sense of belonging and unity, nurturing relationships, and fortifying bonds with those around us.

But what about **bringing about positive change and making a difference**? Again, Paul uses the analogy of the human body in 1 Corinthians 12:12-27 to convey the purpose of spiritual gifts. Just as a body consists of many parts working in unison, isn't it true that we, as a body of believers, are meant to operate harmoniously, valuing each unique gift? Doesn't each part play a vital role in supporting and caring for one another? If one part suffers, doesn't the whole body feel it? And when one part is honoured, don't we all rejoice? No matter how small, each gift has the power to leave a lasting impact. Serving others with our gifts, don't we contribute to the greater good, creating a more compassionate and harmonious world?

Could it be that spiritual gifts also **bring joy and inspiration**? When you share your gifts, you uplift others, infusing their lives with beauty, encouragement, and hope. Is it not true that your gifts, whether a soul-stirring song, a comforting presence, or a word of wisdom, have the power to touch hearts and brighten someone's day?

Remember, the goal behind spiritual gifts isn't to compare or rank them, but to foster unity and build up the body of believers. Whether you have the gift of prophecy or the gift of giving, isn't it true that all gifts are essential and contribute to the collective growth and well-being of the community? Each gift is valuable and serves a unique purpose. Isn't this a beautiful testament to the fact that no gift is superior or inferior, stressing the importance of collaboration and mutual support?

These extraordinary abilities, bestowed by God, cannot be gained through ordinary means. That's why they are called spiritual gifts. They stand as expressions of divine influence and can contribute to the growth and enrichment of the community.

Reflect on a moment when someone acknowledged your exceptional abilities effortlessly. Could this be one of your divine gifts? Jot down your reflections and encounters. Contemplate how you can cultivate and enhance this extraordinary gift for the benefit of others.

____

____

____

____

____

____

____

To finish, let's reflect on this timeless quote from Leo Buscaglia: "**Your talent is God's gift to you. What you do with it is your gift back to God**". Don't forget, your spiritual gifts are not only meant for your personal growth but also for the betterment of the collective. So, why not embrace your gifts, celebrate the unique contributions they bring, and use them to make a positive impact on the world around you?

ACTION STEPS FOR YOU:

Chapter 1 – Unwrapping Your Gift	
Discover your True self	Take the time to think about what a gift really means to you. Explore your passions, interests, and what brings you joy. Remember, your uniqueness is the foundation of your gift, and there is no one else like you!
Unveil your potential	Dive deep into your natural passions and abilities. Recognise that your gift is special and has the potential to transform lives, including yours. Embrace your gift and let it guide you to your true purpose.
Nurture your spiritual side	Look beyond the surface and tap into your spiritual self. Embrace the idea that you are here for a reason and that your gift is an essential part of your journey. Embracing your spirituality can empower you to use your gift for the greater good.

Chapter 2

Navigating Your Journey to Find Your Special Gifts

"Like the sand of the earth, your gifts are countless, and some are stepping on theirs without knowing." - Michael Bassey Johnson

Discovering your special gift isn't as difficult as you may have believed. Have you ever felt like you aren't special or that you don't have any unique talents? Let me reassure you, that's far from the truth. The fact is, you do have distinctive talents and qualities, and these are your gifts. Ready to uncover them? Simply follow the steps shared in this book.

This chapter will walk you through the process of identifying both your natural and spiritual gifts, starting with your natural ones. You might even be surprised to find that you're not just gifted in one area, but several! Usually, one gift will stand out more than the others, but you may certainly use more than one gift, which is why I refer to gifts in the plural.

Remember, the process of discovering natural and spiritual gifts differs significantly. But don't worry, by diligently following the steps outlined in this guide, you'll be able to pinpoint your gifts and start using them to fulfil your life's purpose.

Feeling a bit overwhelmed? Hold on, keep an open mind, and continue exploring your various gifts. With dedication and perseverance, you can uncover your gifts and use them to make a positive change in the world. Ready to get started? Here are the steps to uncover your special gifts.

1. Embracing a Fresh Perspective: Hidden Possibilities

Have you ever wondered about the key to your innate gifts? Could the answer be as simple as embracing a fresh perspective? It's all about cultivating a growth mindset. This involves welcoming learning experiences and viewing setbacks as stepping stones toward success. Isn't it true that a positive outlook can help you flourish while a negative mindset can hold you back?

Let's consider an example. Imagine two individuals: Jane and Sarah. Jane, trapped in a pessimistic mindset, often struggles financially, consumed by her failures and setbacks. On the other hand, Sarah, armed with a growth mindset, has managed to see opportunities in challenges, leading her towards financial prosperity. Can you see the difference?

The power of a growth mindset lies in its core focus on productivity. It allows you to perceive the bright side in every situation and seize the opportunities it presents. Could this be the fundamental step in your quest to unearth your natural gifts? It entails embracing continuous learning, reframing failures as valuable lessons, and maintaining an unwavering positive perspective.

Are you ready to make this shift in your mindset? By doing so, you'll uncover the hidden treasures within you, propelling yourself toward self-discovery and empowerment. Isn't it time you started to truly realise your potential?

2. Unearth Your Potential: A Guided Journey to Discover Strengths, Passions, and Gifts

Let's dive deep into your unique strengths, passions, and gifts. Discovering these personal qualities can be a significant step towards understanding your own value and uniqueness. By identifying and embracing these aspects of yourself, you can leverage them for personal growth and success. So, are you ready to embark on this journey of self-discovery?

Firstly, it's important to find a calm and quiet space that encourages reflection. Have you got a notebook or journal handy? This will be a great tool for jotting down your thoughts and insights during this process, helping you stay present and focused.

To begin, it's crucial to distinguish between your strengths, passions, and gifts. Understanding the difference between these three aspects can guide you in making informed decisions about how to best use each one in your life or career path. So, let's delve into each one.

Strengths: Are there any particular skills or abilities that you naturally excel at? These are areas where you tend to outperform others and feel a sense of confidence.

Passions: What activities or interests truly energize and excite you? These are the things you genuinely enjoy and find rewarding.

Gifts: Can you identify any unique qualities or talents that seem to come effortlessly to you? These could be innate abilities that you can apply in various areas of your life.

Remember, this process is all about uncovering your unique identity and harnessing these qualities for personal growth. Are you ready to get started?

Set aside uninterrupted time for self-reflection. This exercise will consist of three sections: Strengths, Passions, and Gifts. In each section, ask yourself the following questions and record your answers in the chart provided:

The First Step: Identifying your strengths

Let's embark on the first step together – pinpointing your strengths. Consider these questions:

a) Can you recall the activities where you shine, earning compliments and recognition?

b) Are there any tasks or projects that you breeze through with ease and efficiency?

c) Over time, what are the skills you've managed to sharpen and refine?

Take a moment to reflect and jot down at least three personal strengths. Remember, these strengths are your unique abilities, highlighting what you bring to the table.

MY STRENGTHS	
Questions	**Answers**
What activities do I excel at?	
What tasks feel effortless?	
What skills have I developed?	

Do you remember a cherished childhood hobby of yours? Maybe, like me, you had a passion for games that involved problem-solving. Ever noticed how these early passions often point to our innate talents? In my case, it set the stage for a fulfilling career in numbers and analytical tasks. Have you had a similar experience? If so, why not jot it down?

Let's be honest here, it's crucial to identify and note down the things you genuinely excel at. Ever considered seeking help from your family and friends in this discovery process? They often observe you in your element, noticing skills and strengths you might overlook. When did they last see you shine? What did they notice? Why not ask them and note down their insights? You can approach them individually or as a group, whichever works best for you.

____

____

____

____

____

____

____

Remember, you're not jotting down your passions, but your strengths. What are some things you've excelled at? Perhaps you've won accolades or received praise for them? Once you've compiled a list, cross-check it with the feedback you've received from your loved ones. Noticed any overlaps? Highlight them. Anything missing? Add it in.

Let me share a personal experience. I asked three family members to pinpoint my strongest attribute. Though I asked for a single word, they painted a vivid picture using multiple adjectives. One word, however, was a recurring theme: sociable. Intrigued, I probed further. Turns out, they see me as a social butterfly, someone who thrives in the company of others. This, they believe, is my unique gift.

Now, how about you? What's your unique gift, according to your loved ones? And does it align with your own perception of your strengths?

The Second Step: Discovering your passions

Moving on to the second step, let's delve into the exploration of your passions:

a) Are there any activities or hobbies that light up your face with joy and excitement?

b) Imagine this - if you had limitless time and resources, where would you direct your energy and focus?

c) Are there certain topics or causes that stir a strong feeling in you, as if igniting a fire within your soul?

Take some time to ponder over these questions and jot down at least three passions that emerge from your thoughts. Let's journey together to discover what truly ignites your heart.

MY PASSIONS	
Questions	**Answers**
What activities bring me joy?	
What would I do with unlimited time and resources?	
What topics ignite a fire within me?	

Are you finding this task a bit challenging? Try taking a nostalgic journey back to your childhood. Can you remember what you loved doing most? Were you into singing, playing an instrument, or perhaps expressing yourself through drawing? Did you dream of wearing a white coat and saving lives, or donning a suit and running a business, or even breaking records as an athlete? Take a moment to jot down these memories.

The Third Step: Discovering your natural gifts

Moving on to the third step, let's delve into the realm of your natural gifts.

a) Consider the unique qualities that others often applaud in you. What are those special talents that people readily acknowledge in you?

b) Reflect on the activities you perform with ease, almost effortlessly. What are the tasks you engage in without needing much practice or exerting much effort?

c) Identify the tasks that you naturally excel at. What are the activities that just seem to flow naturally for you?

Please take a moment to identify at least three natural gifts that you believe you possess. Remember, this is about recognising your innate abilities and potential.

MY NATURAL GIFTS	
Questions	**Answers**
What unique qualities or abilities do others acknowledge in me?	
What do I effortlessly do well?	
What comes naturally to me?	

Now that you've put some thought into it, let's take it a step further. Using the table below, identify those qualities that appear to be your most prominent strengths, passions, and gifts.

This exercise is not just about listing your gifts, but also understanding why you gravitate towards certain activities. Reflecting on how these inclinations have manifested since your childhood can provide a deeper understanding of your natural gifts. So, are you ready to embark on this journey of self-discovery?

Note: Either write on this book or grab a blank piece of paper and let's get to work. What are your strengths? What are your passions? What unique gifts do you bring to the table? Don't be shy – pen them down.

Remember, this is just the beginning. It's a process that requires your time, exploration, and patience to truly understand and embrace the wonderful qualities you possess. And as you delve deeper, don't forget to trust your intuition and enjoy every step of the journey.

As you start understanding yourself better, you'll find the confidence to pursue a life that is perfectly aligned with your true self. Isn't that an exciting prospect?

3. Discovering You: Get Insights from Quizzes

The Benefits of Personality Tests

Are you struggling to pinpoint your unique strengths and define your purpose in life? If so, you're not alone – and there are tools out there that can help. Have you considered taking online quizzes and tests? They're designed to help you identify your strengths and could offer you some seriously valuable insights. There are various types available, from personality type quizzes and character strengths assessments to Purpose Quotient evaluations.

My Personal Experience with Tests

Have you ever tried taking a self-discovery test? Have you ever considered what your personal work style might reveal about you? Let me tell you about a fascinating experience I once had at a workshop. After responding to a set of questions, I received an **Insights Discovery**[1] profile. Can you imagine how enlightening it was to receive a clear framework that guided my self-awareness and personal growth journey?

Reading my profile, would you be surprised to learn that I have a systematic and organised thinking style, coupled with highly developed analytical skills? That's right! It merely affirmed what I already knew about myself.

Now, wouldn't it make sense for someone with these traits to work with digital systems, databases, reporting tools, and visual dashboards? Indeed, it does! And, as you might have guessed, I am professionally known as an Analyst. Do you see how understanding your work style can confirm what you already know and guide you in your professional journey? How well do you think your profession aligns with your personal traits?

Remember when we started this book and I gave you the chance to take one of the straightforward quizzes – **"How Empowered Are You?"** – that I created to ascertain your current strengths? There will be another one available at the end of the book.

Because I can personally see the value in self-discovery tests, I went as far as creating my own personality tests. Though I initially crafted these quizzes for my own benefit as I wanted to tap into the power within me and inspire my journey of transformation, I found these to be a useful tool as a starting point to that journey. These simple quizzes were designed specifically to help get a sneak peek into your strengths, sparking your interest to dig deeper into discovering your core strengths. By understanding these strengths and utilising them to their fullest extent, you can unleash the full power of your potential.

If you haven't taken the first quiz yet on empowerment, how about giving it a try? I wholeheartedly encourage you to do so and get a deeper understanding of your current level of empowerment.

Once you have taken the quiz, you will receive your empowerment score and a personalised message to inspire your journey of transformation. In chapter 7 of this book, you will find the extended description of each empowerment score.

And in the final pages of this book, your answers to the **"What is Your Special Gift?"** quiz – if you choose to complete it – will provide valuable insights into your unique gift and the potential impact you can create in the world. Similarly to the empowerment quiz results, you will find the extended description of each type of unique gift at the end of the section.

Interpreting Your Results

Ever wondered how well you really know yourself? You might be surprised at the insights you could gain from taking a personality test. Yes, it's true that their accuracy isn't always perfect, but they might just give you a clearer picture of your strengths. If you're someone who struggles with self-reflection or lacks a close-knit circle of friends to provide feedback, these tests can be particularly beneficial.

Have you ever heard of the **16Personalities**[2] test? It's a free online tool that many businesses and NGOs (non-governmental organizations) hold in high regard. Based on the Myers-Briggs Type Indicator, it delves into various personality types and how they affect our work, communication, and teamwork. When I took the test, I was astounded by how precise it described me. My result? An Extraverted, iNtuitive (this is not a typo), Feeling, Judging type, known as ENFJ or, alternatively, the "Insightful Contributor" or Protagonist.

Curious about what that means? Here's a little glimpse from the 16Personalities website describing the Protagonist personality type:

“Protagonists (ENFJs) feel called to serve a greater purpose in life. Thoughtful and idealistic, these personality types strive to have a positive impact on other people and the world around them. They rarely shy away from an opportunity to do the right thing, even when doing so is far from easy.

Protagonists are born leaders, which explains why these personalities can be found among many notable politicians, coaches, and teachers. Their passion and charisma allow them to inspire others not just in their careers but in every area of their lives, including their relationships. Few things bring Protagonists a deeper sense of joy and fulfilment than guiding friends and loved ones to grow into their best selves.”

So, why not consider taking the test and discover your unique personality traits? You might just uncover some surprising strengths along the way.

Exploring Your Personality Type

As a dedicated coach, my passion is seeing you succeed. How about we delve into your unique abilities and strengths? Have you considered participating in a workshop or a training session? These are carefully designed to leverage my robust coaching and teaching skills for your benefit. I challenge you to take an online quiz, could there be some truth in its results? This could be a valuable tool to uncover your personal strengths and guide your path to personal development.

Using Personality Tests as a Tool

Let me assure you, personality tests can be a potent tool on your journey to self-discovery. But remember, these tests are not the ultimate truth or a rigid blueprint for your life. They serve as a helpful starting point. What if you approach them with an open mind, ready to explore and ponder? Do the results echo your life experiences and future dreams? Allow these tests to guide you, but never let them define you.

The Continuous Journey of Self-Discovery

How well do you know your own strengths and life purpose? Have you ever considered blending the insights from personality tests with deep self-reflection and real-life experiences? This can be a powerful tool for understanding yourself at a deeper level. It's all about continual growth and evolution, don't you agree? Now, if this method doesn't resonate with you, don't worry. There are other paths you can take to uncover your unique strengths. Remember, this journey of self-discovery never ends.

4. The Power of Praise: Listening to the Good

Do you remember a time when you had the chance to help a colleague navigate a challenging situation? Just like you, I've been there too. During a leadership course, I found myself in a position to lend a helping hand to a struggling peer. Although I won't go into the nitty-gritty of their issue, I was tasked with asking probing questions and offering valuable insights that would help them see things from a new angle. The aim? To help them discover a solution or consider different strategies. I threw myself wholeheartedly into this coaching role.

Can you imagine how taken aback I was when, after the training, I received an unexpected message from the Head of department who had been facilitating the session? She praised my inquisitiveness and reflection, even suggesting that I had a natural talent for coaching. Have you ever been complimented in such a way that it made you view yourself in a new light?

And guess what? Her message didn't end there. She went on to express her confidence in my potential as a coach and the positive impact I could make in a field that desperately needs guidance. How would you react to such encouraging words?

You see, when seasoned professionals in your field take the time to notice your abilities, it is vital to sit up and listen! Why, you ask? Because their feedback can expose the hidden potential within you that you may have overlooked. Isn't it amazing that sometimes it takes another person to reveal the greatness within us?

5. Taking the Leap: From Lists to Purposeful Steps

Ready to make the leap from simply listing your strengths and passions to actively using them? Let's explore how you can manifest your gifted self through purposeful action!

What steps can you take? The key lies in making the most of your strengths and passions. Review your list and identify the ones that you can start leveraging right away. Perhaps it's your ability to give, to encourage others, to show kindness, to smile or to show bravery. In the meantime, you can work on nurturing other gifts, which we'll discuss in the next section.

Are you feeling overwhelmed with a long list of strengths and passions? Don't worry. Simplify things by focusing on your most powerful strengths and passions first. If there are other areas that you're passionate about and can't bear to let go, give them a test run. But remember, avoid burning yourself out by taking on too much too quickly.

Here's another strategy to narrow down your options. Consider what you can uniquely engage in, given your current circumstances. For example, as a busy mother, you might find that small, meaningful acts of kindness are something you can excel at, even with your bustling schedule. Why not take advantage of those quiet moments early in the morning or during nap times to write encouraging notes to slip into your children's lunchboxes or to leave for a neighbour who might need a boost? Or perhaps you prefer those late-night moments when the house is finally quiet. Use these opportunities to donate a few items to a local food bank through an online platform or to send a quick message of support to a friend.

Don't put off spreading kindness until your children are older or until you have more free time. Instead, seize the moment and nurture your habit of making small but impactful gestures that brighten someone's day.

On the other hand, if you're drawn to a more time-consuming or resource-intensive activity like starting a business or an intensive training program, it's key to be realistic about the demands. Consider smaller scale or more manageable ways to nurture that strength, such as online courses, local networking groups, or incorporating your interest into your existing routines. As a busy mom, embracing your strengths lets you find fulfilment and personal growth amidst the unique challenges and joys of motherhood.

Once you've prioritised your strengths and passions, start working on the ones that stand out the most or that may not be feasible later in life. But remember, don't just give them a short trial period and then abandon them, unless you're unsure if they're truly your gifts. Instead, visualise a future where your gifts are integrated into your everyday life. Remember, utilising your gifts not only creates opportunities but also brings fulfilment and success.

6. Embracing the Gift Within: Unwrapping Spiritual Insights

Each one of us has unique spiritual gifts, waiting to be discovered and used for our fulfilment and purpose. If you're eager to unwrap these gifts and harness their power, let me guide you through the key steps on this life-changing journey.

Adopt a new perspective

Your journey to receiving your spiritual gifts begins with opening your mind to new possibilities that dwell within you. It's about embracing a mindset that's receptive to the spiritual world and the potential it holds. Can you acknowledge that there is a force greater than you at play? By doing so, you create room for your spiritual gifts to come alive.

Picture this: a woman yearning for a deeper purpose in life. She starts by nurturing a sense of curiosity and awe, delving into various spiritual practices, and striving to connect with her inner self. Along the way, she notices a shift in her consciousness, understanding that a higher power is steering her path. How about embracing this new perspective, just like her, and opening yourself to receive your spiritual gifts?

Invite the divine presence into your life

Have you ever thought about inviting divine presence into your life? This isn't just about acknowledging a higher power, but it's about aligning yourself with the guidance of this power. By doing this, you create a sacred space in your heart and spirit, where your spiritual gifts can be revealed.

Does the phrase "**Ask and you will receive, seek and you will find, knock and the door will be opened to you**" sound familiar to you? This profound wisdom comes from the Bible, specifically from the book of Matthew, chapter 7, verses 7-8. These verses are about persistence and faith in seeking spiritual guidance and blessings.

What does it really mean? Let's explore this further together:

a) "**Ask and it will be given to you**". What does this mean to you? Consider the power of prayer and communication with the divine. By reaching out and expressing your desires, needs and intentions, you open the channel for receiving spiritual gifts. It's about seeking a deeper connection with the divine and being open to receiving its blessings.

b) What about **"Seek and you will find"**? It underscores the importance of actively searching and exploring. It encourages you to delve into your spiritual growth, seek knowledge, and embrace practices that align with your inner quest. As you seek, you create opportunities for your spiritual gifts to be revealed and for your understanding to expand.

c) And finally, **"Knock and the door will be opened to you"**. This suggests the act of approaching and engaging with the divine. It's your willingness to knock on the door of divine wisdom and guidance, seeking entry into a deeper spiritual realm. By knocking, you demonstrate your readiness to embrace spiritual gifts and invite divine intervention into your life.

Let's consider Barbara, for instance. She's hoping to invite God's presence into her life. Can you relate to her? You, like Barbara, can engage in practices such as meditation, prayer or contemplation. Connect with the divine energy that resonates with you, namely the Spirit of God (or the Holy Spirit), as referenced in the Bible. Through these practices, express your intention to receive your spiritual gifts and open yourself humbly to divine grace.

Remember, through these practices of persistent inquiry and seeking, you uncover the treasures that lie within you. So, are you ready to tap into the wellspring of your spiritual gifts and talents, allowing them to flourish and positively impact your life and those around you?

Imagine yourself tapping into your spiritual gifts and talents, allowing them to flourish and positively impact both your life and the lives of others. You can approach your spiritual journey with faith, perseverance, and a genuine desire to align yourself with the divine purpose and blessings that await you.

Cultivate Awareness and Receptivity

Have you ever considered the power of cultivating awareness and receptivity in your daily life? It is the key to unlocking your spiritual gifts. How, might you wonder? It all boils down to being more open and aware, noticing the subtle signs, synchronicities, and intuitive nudges that are guiding you towards your gifts. What if you could create the perfect environment for your gifts to manifest, simply by being fully present and mindful?

Consider this. Perhaps you've always had a deep love for singing or reading poetry. You've felt the profound impact music and words can have, touching the very souls of people, offering solace, comfort, healing, and joy. But have you ever thought about the role of awareness and receptivity in this creative realm? It's not just about technical skills or crafting perfect rhymes, is it? It's about truly understanding and connecting with the emotions, experiences, and needs of your audience.

How can you achieve this? As a singer or poet, you'll want to foster deep empathy and compassion. Have you taken the time to observe and listen to the world around you, noticing the struggles, joys, and desires people carry within? By doing so, you can develop an acute awareness of the human condition and the universal emotions that bind us all.

What about using your singing or poetry to bring comfort to those who are hurting? You can select songs or write verses that resonate with themes of hope, resilience, and the human spirit's triumph. Imagine your music or words being a gentle embrace, a reminder to those in tough times that they are not alone.

And what about bringing joy and upliftment? By selecting uplifting melodies or crafting verses that evoke happiness and inspiration, your performances or written pieces could become a source of positivity and encouragement. Can you see how your work could create moments of shared delight and enthusiasm?

In times of sorrow or grief, have you considered using your singing or poetry as a healing tool? Your voice or words could offer a soothing balm, providing a safe space for people to express their emotions and find comfort in shared experiences. Your songs or poems could act as a catharsis, helping individuals navigate their pain and find inner peace.

By dedicating yourself to cultivating awareness and receptivity, you'll become more attuned to your audience's needs and preferences. Are you actively seeking feedback and engaging in dialogue with those who resonate with your work? By listening to their stories, experiences, and feedback, their insights can shape your future creations.

And as you refine your craft and deepen your understanding of music or poetry's power, you'll start to see that your unique gifts have the potential to touch and transform lives. Can you see how by sharing your voice or words with authenticity, vulnerability, and compassion, you can become an instrument of peace, joy, comfort, healing, and solace for others?

This is the power of cultivating awareness and receptivity in the realm of singing or poetry. Through immersing yourself in the human experience, understanding the power of music or words, and creating with empathy and intention, you open up opportunities for connection, healing, and transformation through your artistic expression. Does this resonate with you?

Nurture and Use your Gifts

Discovering your spiritual gifts is only the first step! Like a seed needing care to flourish into a beautiful plant, your gifts demand your attention, active engagement, and development. Let's illustrate this concept with an example.

Consider Stephanie's story. She's on a unique journey to explore her innate gift of creating harmonious and healing environments. She's recognised her ability to transform spaces in ways that bring comfort, inspiration, and tranquillity to those who experience them. So, how does she nurture this gift? Stephanie delves into interior design, focusing on creating spaces that cater to both physical and emotional well-being.

Stephanie begins by mastering the principles of design, such as colour theory and spatial arrangement. Imagine her using soft, calming colours and strategically placed furniture to create soothing environments where people can relax and recharge. But that's not all. Stephanie also explores the role of natural elements, incorporating plants and natural light to enhance the overall atmosphere of her designs. She appreciates how these elements can positively influence mood and stress levels – don't you?

Pushing her boundaries even further, Stephanie delves into the therapeutic effects of layout and design on mental health. Picture her crafting spaces that foster a sense of peace and safety, perhaps creating cosy corners for reflection or vibrant areas that inspire creativity and joy. Whether it's through thoughtful furniture placement or the integration of calming sounds, she brings a healing touch to her environments.

Have you ever felt the profound impact of a thoughtfully, well-designed room can have on emotional well-being? Stephanie certainly has. She integrates mindfulness into her design practice, using her keen awareness to ensure that every space promotes a sense of balance and harmony. Through her compassionate and intentional design choices, Stephanie becomes a source of comfort and inspiration for those who experience her work.

As she nurtures her gift, Stephanie keeps exploring other aspects of design that resonate with her, like sustainable materials and eco-friendly practices. As she actively incorporates these elements, she not only enhances her own well-being but also becomes a beacon of positive change in her community.

It's important to remember that nurturing and using your gift involves exploring a myriad of modalities and approaches. It's about adopting different tools and techniques that align with your unique abilities and passions. Through thoughtful design, mindfulness, and a deep understanding of environmental impact – as well as through touch, words, music, art, counselling, and similar methods – you too can unlock the full potential of your gift and make a profound difference in others’ lives.

In Chapter 6 of this book, we'll dive deeper into how you can nurture and use your unique gifts. So, stay tuned for more enlightening insights and practical advice on how to maximise your spiritual gifts.

Insights from Those Who Know You

Have you ever considered the transformative power of your spiritual gifts? They can bring a profound depth and purpose to your life. Opening up to the possibilities these divine gifts offer is an empowering journey, and who better to guide you along this path than those who know you best?

Instead of focusing solely on identifying your gifts, how about creating an inviting space within yourself to fully receive them? Engaging in meaningful conversations with your trusted friends might help you understand the gifts they see in you, and how to nurture these gifts.

Why not start a discussion with a close friend about your spiritual gifts? Consider having open and honest discussions, where you can express your desire to explore and fully receive these divine blessings. Encourage them to share what qualities and talents they see in you. Their unique viewpoint, shaped by their experiences with you, can provide valuable insights into the gifts that may already be blossoming in your life.

For example, what if a friend admires your ability to bring tranquillity and comfort to others through your caring presence and soothing words?

Acknowledging and nurturing this gift could potentially expand its impact and bring even greater peace and happiness to those around you.

While the opinions of others are valuable, don't forget that the real acceptance of your gifts lies within your own experiences and inner intuition. Have you put aside time for self-reflection and observation? Take notice of moments when you feel profound joy and alignment with your higher purpose, as they are confirmations of the gifts flowing through you.

Remember, the process of receiving and embracing your spiritual gifts is a transformative journey that demands openness and receptivity. Engaging in conversations with your trusted friends, irrespective of their religious beliefs, can deepen your understanding. Whether it's discussions with any close friend or seeking guidance from Christian friends, embrace the nurturing and receiving process with gratitude and intention. Allow the wisdom and support of those who know you well to guide you, as you unlock the boundless potential of your spiritual gifts.

Cultivating Patience and Perseverance

Envision your journey as a garden in bloom. It has seasons of growth and moments of dormancy, but each phase is vital to the garden's overall beauty. View setbacks as moments of pruning and tending. Just as a gardener's care brings forth the most vibrant blossoms, your challenges and setbacks can lead to your most significant growth.

Embrace the Journey with Curiosity and Courage

Embracing your journey is like embarking on a thrilling expedition. Your gift is a lantern, casting light not only on your personal journey but also acting as a beacon for others in their quest. Are you brave enough to step forward with an open heart, curiosity and courage? Imagine yourself as a torchbearer, illuminating the world around you.

The road may be filled with unexpected twists and turns, but isn't the promise of a life filled with purpose and fulfilment worth every step you take? Seize the day, embrace your journey, and uncover the awe-inspiring treasure that is your life.

ACTION STEPS FOR YOU:

Chapter 2 - Navigating Your Journey to Find Your Special Gift	
Cultivate a growth mindset	Believe that you can find and develop your special gift. Embrace a growth mindset that sees challenges as opportunities for growth and learning. Trust in your ability to grow and discover your true potential.
Recognise your strengths	Conduct a sincere self-analysis to identify your strengths. Embrace your unique qualities, skills and experiences. Remember that your strengths are the building blocks of your gift and can lead you to meaningful discoveries.
Pay attention to feedback	Listen to what others are saying about you and be open to feedback. Sometimes others can see our gifts more clearly than ourselves. Let their comments guide you to a better understanding of your gifts.

References made in Chapter 2

1. **Insights Discovery website:**
   https://www.insights.com/products/insights-discovery/

2. **16Personalities website:**
   https://www.16personalities.com/

Chapter 3

Nurture Your Gift: Let It Shine!

"No one respects a talent that is concealed." - Desiderius Erasmus

Have you ever taken the time to really explore and appreciate the unique gifts that you possess, both innate and spiritual? It's worth taking a moment to do so. Think about how you've been using these gifts. Have you been nurturing them, helping them grow and develop, or have they been left dormant, untouched and unappreciated?

Remember, having a gift is just the beginning. It's how you develop and refine these talents that truly matters. Neglecting or misusing your gift can be detrimental, not just to you, but to those around you as well. Let's work towards cultivating your gifts, refining them to their highest potential.

As we've previously touched upon, we discussed how investing your time and effort into your gifts can lead to their more effective utilisation. By dedicating yourself to growing these gifts, you can unlock their full potential and put them to service for the benefit of others.

So, I urge you to ponder on this. Consider your unique gifts and how you can further develop them. Let's not let your talents be wasted or hidden away. Be the force of change in the world by embracing and refining your gifts with determination and compassion. Remember, your unique abilities can bring joy and uplift those around you. Let's put them to good use.

1. The Power of Nurturing: Unveiling the Impact of Ignoring Your Gifts

What possible impact could occur if you ignored your talents and abilities? Allow me to share some inspiring biblical narratives and real-life stories, which, regardless of your beliefs, can resonate with you and provide some food for thought.

Take, for instance, the story of Joseph. He possessed the unique gift of interpreting dreams. When he shared his dreams with his brothers, jealousy reared its ugly head, and they sold him into slavery. Even in the face of adversity and imprisonment, Joseph never buried his gift. Do you see the power of trust in his abilities? This trust ultimately elevated him to a position of power where he could use his gift to save countless lives during a famine.

You can also draw inspiration from David. His gift of music and leadership was instrumental in his life's journey. As a young shepherd, he honed his musical talent, which went on to soothe King Saul's troubled spirit. Can you imagine how David's gift not only transformed his life but also led him to become a wise and brave king with a profound connection with God?

Now, let's consider Mother Teresa, a woman whose heart overflowed with compassion and empathy. She devoted her life to serving the most impoverished and marginalized in society. Can you see how her gift of empathy and selfless love inspired numerous individuals to band together to improve the lives of those in need?

And who can forget the legendary Maya Angelou? Despite tremendous challenges, Maya never shied away from speaking her truth and advocating for equality and justice. Do you see how her powerful words and activism have motivated generations and left a lasting impression on the world?

From these stories, do you see the compelling lessons we can learn about the consequences of using or ignoring our gifts? It's not just about personal success. Embracing and developing your gifts can make a significant difference in others' lives and the world.

Showcasing your talents, whilst feeling uncertain about their worth, is a common fear that can hinder us from making the positive impact we're capable of. Just like Joseph's brothers who failed to see his potential, others may not always understand the depth of your talents. But should that stop you from growing and using your gifts? Absolutely not!

When you bury your talents, what happens? You miss opportunities, you don't live up to your full potential, and your life may lack fulfilment. By not embracing and developing your talents, you're robbing yourself of the chance to make a significant contribution to society, causing a disconnection from your purpose.

But what if you choose to nurture your gifts instead? These can open doors to opportunities and lead you to paths of significance. Remember how David's music calmed King Saul? Your talents can have a similar positive effect on others, bringing comfort, joy and inspiration.

I hope you're beginning to see that we each have unique talents, and it's not just about skill, but the immense capacity we have to change the lives of those around us. Our talents aren't meant to be hidden but shared with the world.

To develop your talents, it will take courage, determination, and perseverance, just like Maya Angelou who stood against injustice. You too, have to be ready to face challenges when using your talents for a greater purpose.

As women seeking to find our life's purpose, we must understand that our talents aren't confined to specific roles or positions. We may not all be world leaders or famous figures, but each one of us can make a difference right where we are.

Take, for instance, Maria's story. She had a gift for empathy and counselling but didn't see its worth and buried it under societal pressure. However, when she used her gift to help a colleague, she realised her true calling and decided to use her talent to bring healing and hope to people's lives.

Maria's story emphasises the importance of embracing and developing our talents. When we bury them, we not only deny ourselves fulfilment, but also withhold unique contributions from the world. Like Maria, your talents are meant to serve a purpose and positively affect those around you.

Can you see yourself in any of these stories? Are you a new mother, a businesswoman embarking on a new venture, a single woman on a self-discovery journey, a student unsure about the future, or a retiree seeking new meaning in life? Regardless of your stage in life, your talents hold a tremendous potential for impact.

Let's make a commitment to dig up our talents, nurture them, and use them for good. As we do, we'll experience the joy of living a life without burying our talents – a life filled with purpose, fulfilment, and positive influence. The world needs your talents, and you're meant to shine brightly, making it a better place for all. Embrace your talents and let them guide you towards a life of purpose and empowerment.

2. Embracing Your Riches: The Rewards of Developing Your Gifts

The unique gifts and talents that you possess are like hidden treasures, waiting to be discovered and cherished. These are the riches that lie within you. When you tap into these, not only do you grow personally, but you also become a positive influence on those around you. I invite you to look at the inspiring women from the Bible, to understand the importance of acknowledging and using your gifts instead of keeping them hidden.

Consider Esther, for instance. Despite daunting obstacles, she employed her bravery and knowledge to safeguard her people. Doesn't her story illustrate how employing our talents, especially in difficult times, can bring about significant change in other's lives?

Then there's Deborah, celebrated for her leadership and insightfulness. With fearlessness, she steered her people towards peace and prosperity. Her legacy shows how effectively using your gifts can leave a deep, positive impact on those you serve.

By suppressing your talents, aren't you missing out on chances for self-improvement and achievement? Imagine having a priceless jewel but keeping it concealed in the dark. Isn't it meant to radiate and illuminate your surroundings?

Remember, your gifts are an integral part of you, irrespective of your beliefs. Recognising and nurturing them is akin to finding your life's mission and unlocking your true potential. As women striving for fulfilment, don't we owe it to ourselves to explore and hone our talents?

Each of us holds unique talents waiting to be unearthed, be it in leadership, creativity, compassion, or problem-solving. Don't let doubt or fear deter you. Developing your gifts will empower you to become the best version of yourself and make a meaningful impact on the world.

So, let's draw inspiration from the stories of these courageous women in the Bible who discovered and embraced their gifts. By nurturing our own gifts, can't we too become the best versions of ourselves, unlock our purpose, and lead lives of significance? Remember, your gifts are invaluable, and the world is waiting for them to shine brightly.

3. Unveiling the Blueprint: Ways to Nurture Your Gift

Let's dive into the development of your main gift. You may ask, "How can I possibly develop my gift?" The answer lies in one word: Practice. Yes, it's that simple, but requires commitment. Regular practice is a must, and it may sometimes feel like a sacrifice, but remember, without sacrifice, there can be no victory.

There's a thought-provoking adage that states:

"Practice is winning. If you practice more than anybody else, you will beat everybody else."

How profound is that? So, what's the key to developing your natural gift? You guessed it, practice and apply it where necessary.

When you first uncover your gift, don't expect a massive reward. Your first steps should be about giving your gift freely or expecting little in return. This is a crucial stage in nurturing your talent.

For example, do you believe teaching is your main gift? You could start by assisting children in your community with their studies or offer guidance as a mentor. Have you considered applying for a teaching role in a school or educational organisation? This could be a perfect platform to share your knowledge and make a difference in students' lives. If your gift is giving, start small and gradually increase your generosity over time.

Reflecting on my personal journey, I was adept with databases and numbers as an Analyst. But this wasn't just because I studied it. I always found myself drawn towards games where I had to solve problems or enigmas. However, I only excelled through consistent practice. Even with a natural affinity for it since childhood, regular practice was key to honing my skills. This routine helped me identify and learn from my mistakes, leading to improvement.

So, how can you develop your gift? It's all about work and finding opportunities to apply your talent. Start practicing as much as possible. I'll be sharing more about this in the chapters to come.

Summing up, nurturing your natural talent demands practice and persistence. Begin by giving freely of your gift, expecting little or no reward, and gradually increase your contribution. With consistent practice and effort, you can refine your skills, opening doors to wonderful opportunities in the future.

4. Together We Thrive: Developing Your Gift with Allies

Has it ever crossed your mind how much more you could achieve with some help from your family and friends in developing your unique gift? They can be your strongest allies in this journey. They can offer a safe space for you to explore, grow, and even stumble, as you learn to master your gift. How have you involved your loved ones in your journey so far?

Remember that feedback is a crucial part of growth. Have you considered sharing your experiences and dreams with them? It's a strategy I've personally found useful. For instance, I used to have recurring dreams that would later come to life. By sharing these with my friends, I was able to understand them better and identify patterns. Could something similar work for you?

A journal is another incredibly useful tool. It helps you keep a record of your dreams and track your progress. Have you tried it yet?

In your journey of developing your gift, you might find yourself discovering related talents. Have you thought about seeking guidance from experienced practitioners in your community? Their insights could prove invaluable.

Keep in mind that perfecting your gift is a process, and it takes time. Are you giving yourself the patience and persistence this journey requires?

And finally, why not make the most of opportunities to share your gift with others? This not only helps you refine your skills, but also provides you with invaluable feedback. Can you see how the support from your family and friends can propel you to reach your full potential and create a positive impact in the world? Your journey starts now.

5. Lessons from Setbacks: Turning Failures into Stepping Stones

Setbacks and failures may seem like roadblocks on your journey to success, don't they? But what if you considered them as stepping stones instead? This shift in perspective can propel you forward on your personal journey of self-discovery and growth.

Think about it. Could your setbacks be lessons rather than defeats? They can provide you with invaluable insights, helping you refine your gift and develop resilience. Do you know that even the most accomplished individuals faced failures on their way to greatness?

Let's take the story of J.K. Rowling, the world-renowned author of the "Harry Potter" series. Did you know that before her books became a global sensation, Rowling faced numerous rejections from publishers? Not to mention her personal challenges, including financial hardships. But did she allow these setbacks to deter her? No. She treated each rejection as a stepping stone to refine her craft and make her work even better. Rowling's resilience and determination turned her setbacks into a legendary success story, inspiring millions of readers worldwide.

So, when you face setbacks while nurturing your gift, could you see them as opportunities to refine your approach? Maybe your initial attempt didn't get the outcome you hoped for. Reflect on what worked and what didn't, and use this knowledge to refine your strategy.

Let's look at Serena Williams, the iconic tennis player. Despite her incredible talent, she faced challenges, injuries, and unexpected losses throughout her career. But did she let those setbacks define her? No, she used each setback as a learning opportunity, allowing her to adapt and come back even stronger. Her journey symbolises the power of turning failures into stepping stones.

Setbacks can also serve to strengthen your resilience. Can you see them as part of your growth process? Much like a tree's roots grow deeper in response to wind and storms, setbacks can deepen your determination and resilience in the face of adversity.

Moreover, setbacks can help you recognise your true passion and commitment. When you face obstacles, you can use it as an opportunity to question whether you are truly passionate about what you are pursuing. If your desire remains unwavering despite setbacks, isn't that a clear sign that you are on the right path?

Remember, your journey in nurturing your gift isn't linear; it's a series of steps forward, backward, and sideways. When you face setbacks, could you view them as a chance to learn, adjust, and keep moving forward? Many of the world's most successful individuals credit their failures as crucial elements of their success stories.

As you navigate through setbacks and failures, remember they are essential chapters in your growth story. Are you ready to embrace the lessons they offer and let them guide you towards becoming the empowered, gifted individual you are destined to be? After all, a diamond shines brightest after enduring pressure, and setbacks can highlight the splendour of your gift in unexpected ways.

In the words of the media mogul Oprah Winfrey, "Challenges are gifts that force us to search for a new centre of gravity. Do not fight them. Just find a different way to stand." So, when setbacks come your way, can you stand tall, adjust your stance, and continue your journey of transformation? After all, your setbacks are not roadblocks; they're stepping stones leading to your full potential.

ACTION STEPS FOR YOU:

Chapter 3 - Nurture Your Gift: Let It Shine!	
Understand the cost of inaction	Recognise that burying your gifts can lead to dissatisfaction and regret. Take a moment to imagine your life fully developed with your gift - the joy, impact and fulfilment it brings. Use this vision as motivation to take action and develop your gift.
Reward yourself along the way	Celebrate every step of your gift building journey. Whether it is a small accomplishment or a significant step forward, recognise and reward yourself. Positive reinforcement keeps you motivated and engaged in the process.
Involve your support system	Share your journey with close friends or family members who believe in you. Their encouragement and support can help you stay focused on developing your gift. Remember

that you do not have to do this alone.

Chapter 4

Breaking Free: Overcome the Obstacles to Your Gift

"A great tragedy is to see potentials die unharnessed, but a greater tragedy is to see potentials live but yet untapped." -Dr Myles Munroe

Let's begin this chapter by asking an introspective question. Are you truly utilising your unique gift? If your answer leans towards a 'no', let's delve into why that might be. Have a moment of reflection. You may already have an answer at the tip of your tongue, or perhaps it's still a bit hazy. Regardless, something is undoubtedly hindering you.

If you're uncertain as to why you're not harnessing your gift, there's no need for concern. I'm here to guide you through understanding the potential barriers that may be standing in your way and provide strategies to surmount them.

Recognising what's preventing you from utilising your gift is vital – it's the first step towards unlocking their full potential. Once you've identified the 'whys', you can begin to navigate around these obstacles, and utilise your gifts in ways that not only benefit others but also enrich your own life.

So, here are common obstacles:

1. Fear

Recognising and understanding fear is the first step to overcoming it. Let's explore together the four main types of fear that can prevent us from harnessing our gifts:

The fear of making mistakes

The fear of showing your weaknesses

The fear of experiencing failure or rejection

The fear of being judged

You may have heard that 'FEAR' is often an acronym for:

F – False

E – Evidence

A – Appearing

R – Real

Yes, fear is an illusion, a mere trick of the mind that can grow and hinder us from reaching our true potential.

By understanding each type of fear, we can start to overcome them. For instance, are you hesitating, unsure about using your gifts because you're afraid of making mistakes? Or is the fear of your weaknesses causing you to doubt your abilities? Perhaps you're afraid of failure or rejection, stopping you from taking risks and trying new ventures. Or is it the fear of being judged, making you anxious about how others perceive you?

Recognising these fears and working towards overcoming them is vital for utilising our gifts to the fullest. Remember, fear is just an illusion. With small steps towards our goals, we can conquer it. Are you ready to conquer your fears?

Fear of Making Mistakes

So, you're worried about making mistakes? Well, let me tell you something important - mistakes are a fundamental part of life. We all commit errors and that's perfectly fine. In fact, it's more than fine, it's necessary. How else do we learn and grow?

Now, think about this. You're just embarking on your unique journey, embracing your innate gift. Won't there be some stumbles and missteps along the way? Of course, there will be! But should that stop you from exploring your potential? Absolutely not!

Instead of letting fear of errors paralyse you, why not see it as an exciting part of the journey? Each mistake is a stepping stone, a lesson learned, a chance to refine your talent further.

Remember, nobody is flawless, especially when it comes to new adventures. Should you expect to master your gift overnight? No way! Mastery requires time, patience, and yes, making mistakes.

When you stumble, take a moment to reflect. What can you learn from it? How can you apply that learning next time? This continuous learning cycle is the key to progress, to growing your gift into something truly remarkable.

Think about it this way. Today's mistake is tomorrow's lesson. The earlier you start, the better. Don't let the fear of making mistakes be a barrier. In fact, it's the opposite. It's a catalyst for growth. So, embrace your imperfections, learn from your errors, and watch as you flourish and succeed with your gift.

Fear of Showing Your Weaknesses

Have you ever been afraid to show your weaknesses? It can seem intimidating, can't it? But what if I told you that acknowledging your weaknesses could help you identify your strengths? It's true, your weaknesses are not necessarily a hindrance. They can guide you towards your strengths. The key is to concentrate on your strengths and sharpen them.

We all have strengths and weaknesses, don't we? Sometimes, we are so afraid of being judged for our weaknesses that we don't let our strengths shine through. Other times, we might feel unsatisfied because we're not good at something that's closely related to our strength. Could this fear be holding you back from fully utilising your strengths?

Let's consider a hypothetical scenario. Imagine you have two friends who both have a passion for singing. One is an excellent soprano, while the other is a master of bass. Locally, they have their own fan following, but they're too afraid to take their music careers to the next level. They fear they're not as good as the other. They're focusing more on their limitations rather than their capabilities. Does this sound familiar?

One day, they have a heart-to-heart about their fears and they realise they've been too critical of themselves. They've been comparing themselves to each other rather than valuing their own unique talents. So, they resolve to focus on their individual strengths and it proved to be fruitful. They both found success and their fans adored their unique voices and songs.

This could be your story too if you're focusing more on your weaknesses than your strengths. Remember to concentrate on what you do well. This way, you can overcome this fear and fully utilise your strengths.

Fear of Experiencing Failure or Rejection

Have you ever found yourself paralysed by fear of failure or rejection? Do you often find yourself dwelling on questions like:

"What if I fail?"

“What if I face rejection?”

“What if I’m simply not cut out for this?”

“Is there a chance this won’t work out for me?”

These doubts might seem rational, but they can prevent you from exploring new opportunities and reaching your true potential.

But what if we changed the script in your mind? You have the power to shift your perspective. What if you started asking yourself more optimistic questions?

"What If I succeed?"

"What if I am accepted?"

"What if I am perfect for this?"

"What if I'm exactly what they're looking for?"

"What if this venture does work out for me?"

Can you see how these questions shift your focus towards success and fuel your confidence to step out of your comfort zone?

I understand, sometimes, despite giving your best, you might face failure or rejection. It can be tough dealing with these emotions. But remember, success isn't a walk in the park. It requires consistent effort and time. Failures and rejections are part and parcel of the journey to success. They are not roadblocks, but stepping stones that help you learn and grow.

If you let fear of failure or rejection hold you back, you could be burying your unique gifts. It's crucial to understand that your failures and rejections are not setbacks. They are opportunities for growth and learning. Don't let the fear of failure or rejection deter you from using your gifts. Focus on the positive, embrace the process, and use your gifts to carve your path to success.

So, here's the takeaway for you. Fear of failure and rejection is a common concern that many face. But remember, you have the power to change this narrative. By asking positive questions and understanding that failures and rejections are stepping stones and not setbacks, you can conquer your fears. Don't let these fears stop you from using your gifts and reaching your goals.

Fear of Being Judged

Are you afraid of what others might think about you? Do you often find yourself asking questions like,

"What happens if they discover my mistakes?"

"What if my weaknesses are exposed?"

"Will they laugh at my imperfections?"

or even...

"Would they consider me a failure if I try and fail?"

This fear of judgment can cripple our ability to try new things or to use our gifts. It's discomforting, isn't it? But remember, those who judge or mock you are usually envious of your capabilities.

It's not easy to shake off that feeling, but remember, the ones who ridicule or belittle you are often envious of your abilities. When you stumble upon a mistake or encounter failure while utilising your talent, there will always be people ready to undermine you with negative comments. Often, these are individuals who can't match your skills or perform as well as you. Their criticism and ridicule stem from envy and a desire to be in your shoes.

But remember, there are also those who will always stand by you. They're the ones who will cheer you on, even in tough times. Their support should be your focus, not the fear of judgement from critics.

Let me share a personal experience. When I decided to start my own YouTube channel, I was a 40-year-old new mother with a baby just a few months old, in the midst of a pandemic. My maternity leave felt empty and without purpose. That's when my husband suggested I find a new hobby that could bring me joy and potentially even provide a source of income.

While browsing YouTube, I thought: if other influencers can succeed, why not me? So I started my own channel, focused on late motherhood. However, when I posted my first video, I was consumed by fear of judgement. The video was a short 2-minute clip about a natural remedy for baby constipation. I worried about being dismissed by other mothers and seen as foolish. It took me three weeks to summon the courage to share it with the world.

My husband's wise words helped me overcome my fear. He pointed out that my advice could help other parents soothe their distressed babies. So, despite my apprehensions, I published the video. It took three months to gain traction, but it's now my most popular video, attracting more than a third of my subscribers. And guess what? I now love being on camera and discussing a range of topics!

The lesson here? Embrace Susan Jeffers' advice: "Feel the fear and do it anyway." You never know who you might be helping by sharing your gift.

Now, let's discuss other potential barriers that could be preventing you from utilising your talent. Rest assured, with determination, persistence, and the support of others, you can overcome these hurdles and utilise your gift to benefit others. After all, your gift is meant to be shared with the world. Don't let fear hold you back.

2. Self-Doubt

Are you letting self-doubt overshadow your judgement and limit your potential? Are you familiar with the nagging voice in your mind that raises questions about your abilities, drains your confidence, and fills your mind with uncertainty? Perhaps you live in constant fear of not being good enough or making mistakes, always comparing yourself with others. But let's stop right there. Doubt is not an unconquerable enemy. With a little kindness towards yourself and a lot of determination, you can conquer this demon and unleash the unique gifts that lie within you.

Have you ever realised that self-doubt is nothing more than an illusion created by our minds? It's a common human experience, affecting even the most accomplished individuals. So, when doubts arise, should you berate yourself? No, instead, observe them with curiosity and compassion. Understand that these doubts do not define your worth or abilities. They're just thoughts passing through your consciousness.

But, how can you overcome self-doubt?

Cultivating a positive mindset is a crucial step. Why not focus on your strengths and past successes? Recall the times you overcame challenges and achieved great things. Why not celebrate your unique talents and the qualities that make you special? Engage in positive self-talk and replace self-critical thoughts with affirmations of self-confidence. Try repeating empowering statements like:

"I am capable."

"I have the skills and knowledge to succeed."

"I deserve love and recognition."

Another powerful strategy is to take action. Why not break down your goals into small, manageable steps? When you take action towards your aspirations, you build evidence of your abilities. Every small victory becomes a cornerstone of confidence. So, what's one step you can take today to get closer to using your gifts?

Seeking support from others can also be beneficial. Have you considered sharing your dreams and aspirations with friends, family, or trusted mentors? Surrounding yourself with a community that believes in you can uplift your spirit. Engage in open conversations about self-doubt. You might find comfort in realising that others have faced similar struggles. Remember, you are not alone on this journey.

When self-doubt creeps in, challenge the negative thoughts and beliefs that fuel it. Ask yourself: what evidence do I have that supports these doubts? Are there alternative perspectives that contradict these thoughts? Often, you'll find that self-doubt is based on unfounded assumptions and distorted thought patterns. By questioning and challenging these beliefs, you make room for more empowering and positive narratives.

Viewing failure as an opportunity for growth can also help. Understand that setbacks and mistakes do not reflect your worth or abilities. These are valuable lessons that guide you towards improvement. Embrace a growth mindset, viewing challenges as stepping stones on your journey rather than insurmountable obstacles. Remember, even the most successful people have encountered failures along the way.

In times of doubt, practice self-compassion. Treat yourself with kindness, understanding that everyone faces doubts and insecurities. Be gentle with yourself and leave space for self-care. Cultivate practices that nurture your mind, body, and spirit, such as meditation, journalling, hobbies, or time spent in nature. When you cultivate your overall well-being, you build resilience and open yourself up to new possibilities. Remember, self-doubt is not a permanent state; it is a temporary cloud that can dissipate with time and effort.

Ultimately, the power to overcome self-doubt and use your gifts lies within you. Have faith in your abilities and believe that you deserve success and fulfilment. View challenges as opportunities for growth and never underestimate the impact you can make with your unique talents. The world is waiting for you to share your gifts, and by overcoming self-doubt, you will empower yourself to shine brightly and inspire others along the way. Embrace your journey with courage, compassion, and unwavering faith in yourself. Remember, you are gifted, self-reliant, and capable of achieving greatness.

3. Having a Pessimistic Mindset

Do you often find yourself seeing only the negative aspects of situations? This could be a sign of a pessimistic mindset, and it's something that can hold you back from reaching your full potential. It's not uncommon to let the negative voices in our heads take over, focusing only on the dark aspects and ignoring the bright side. But have you ever wondered why you entertain such pessimistic thoughts?

Your past experiences, upbringing, surroundings, or even a traumatic event can shape your mindset and give you a negative perspective. And when you lend your ear to this negative voice, it only grows stronger, making it even harder for you to see the positive side. Does your inner voice echo thoughts like:

"I can't do it."

"I am not enough."

"I am a loser."

"I can't compete with others because of my circumstances."

"Others are better than me."

"I can't do anything well."

"Life should just be lived, not pushed for."

"My dreams are too big for an average person like me."

These negative thought patterns can be debilitating. But remember, just because you're struggling with a pessimistic mindset now doesn't mean you're doomed to stay that way. We all have the power to change our mindsets, much like we can change our appearances.

Are you one of those people who find it easier to help others than to help themselves? It's time to pay attention to yourself. What kind of thoughts have been dominating your mind lately? It's crucial to recognise and change this mindset so you can fully utilise your unique gifts and talents.

So, how can you start to shift your mindset?

One proven method is through positive self-talk. Your mind, just like your body, needs nourishment. It thrives on positive affirmations that can help you combat negative thoughts and feelings. Why not start each day by telling yourself:

"I am capable, loving, and strong."

"I have amazing gifts and talents."

"I am resourceful."

"I can achieve anything I set my mind to."

"I am unstoppable, unbeatable, and unattainable."

"I am unique and special."

"From now on, I will only entertain positive thoughts."

"I am capable of success."

"I deserve all good things in life."

"Despite my past, I am meant to make a difference and fulfil a purpose."

"I will do this with my unique gifts and abilities."

"May God help me in this journey. Amen."

Why not write these affirmations in a journal and recite them daily? If you consistently feed your mind with positivity, it will soon become an integral part of your thoughts and actions.

And how do you overcome your negative thoughts?

Does that negative voice in your head keep creeping up on you uninvited, trying to bring you down? Well, if you are tired of this, it's time to take charge, and I'm here to guide you. Let's tackle that negative mindset with a bit of fun and strategy, shall we?

The moment that negative voice pops up, it's crucial to silence it immediately. Don't let it nestle into your thoughts like an unwelcome guest. Gather your courage and firmly tell it to leave. Show it that there's no room for negativity in your mind, a place filled with self-belief and positivity.

This next part is a bit of fun. Name that negative voice something you dislike, such as "Mr. Boring" or "Miss Doubtful." Whenever it tries to rain on your parade, sternly tell it off. Imagine yourself scolding it, saying, "Hold it there, Mr. Boring! I'm capable of achieving anything I set my mind to, and success is within my reach!"

Need a little more inspiration? The Bible is a great source. Remember Philippians 4:13, which says:

"I can do all things through Christ who strengthens me."

Keep this verse close and let it remind you of your inner strength.

As you work on silencing those negative thoughts, engage in activities that boost your self-esteem. Ever wanted to try something new but fear held you back? Go for it! Just ensure you prioritise your well-being and avoid unnecessary risks. We want you to flourish, not end up in a risky situation that could've been avoided!

Next up: surround yourself with positive people. It's like adding a dose of sunshine to your life. Seek out those who emit positivity and build strong connections with them. Share your dreams and fears with your family and friends, those who uplift and support you. If your immediate circle lacks positivity, look elsewhere. The gym, your neighbourhood, or work might have people who shine with optimism and a zest for life.

Before you get close to anyone, observe them. Positive people are usually open to new friendships. Their positivity can be sensed in their speech and outlook on life. They engage in productive conversations rather than idle gossip. Their actions and behaviour can tell you a lot about them.

If you're struggling to find positive people, don't worry! Professional counsellors are there to help. They can provide the guidance and tools needed to overcome challenges and foster positivity.

Don't hesitate to ask for help. Remember, you're not alone, and it's okay to seek support.

By surrounding yourself with positive influences and using these tips, you'll be well-equipped to conquer hurdles, boost your confidence, and reveal the amazing person within you. Remember, it's a journey, and it's okay to stumble. Keep going, my friend, and soon you'll be basking in the glow of your own strengths and spreading positivity around you. You can do it!

4. Low Self-Esteem

Do you find yourself constantly battling low self-esteem, feeling like you're not good enough? You're not alone. Many of us struggle with the thought that we're not measuring up to others due to various factors, like an unsupportive upbringing, negative influences, or even traumatic experiences.

Do you find it hard to accept compliments, or are you fretting over minor issues, or are you often overly critical of yourself? These are all signs of low self-esteem, and they can hinder you from realising and utilising your true potential.

Low self-esteem is like having a harsh critic living inside your head. It's like constantly feeling you're unworthy, or that you're not capable, or even that you're not deserving of love. It's a difficult place to be, friend.

So, how can you shift this narrative and improve your self-esteem?

It's not a simple journey, but it's surely possible with determination and patience. The root cause of your low self-esteem could stem from various sources – an unsupportive family environment, traumatic experiences, setbacks, peer pressure, negative influences, or past mistakes. It's crucial to first understand what's at the heart of your low self-esteem so you can begin to address it.

a) Forgiveness

I want to share a heart-to-heart about something that can truly light up your journey to overcoming low self-esteem – forgiving yourself. Picture this as wrapping yourself in a warm, understanding hug.

Is your life taking unexpected turns that seem less than ideal? It happens to us all. Yet, there's a secret weapon at your disposal – forgiveness.

When you forgive yourself, it doesn't mean you're glossing over your mistakes. It means you're acknowledging, "Yes, I've had my share of obstacles, but they are not the compass of the incredible person I am growing into."

Imagine for a moment that you, like every extraordinary individual, are a work of art in motion. Life doesn't come with a user guide, and we all falter at times. But remember, these shortcomings don't lessen your brilliance.

How would it feel to let go of self-blame and step into the liberating space that forgiveness offers? It's akin to whispering to yourself, "I deserve love and respect, with all my flaws included."

Do you know where confidence truly blossoms? In the fertile soil of self-compassion. So, when past mistakes attempt to darken your glow, take a deep breath and opt for self-forgiveness. You're still growing, and that's the beautiful journey of being genuinely you.

In the vast tableau of life, your struggles are but minuscule brush strokes in a much larger masterpiece. It's not about erasing them; it's about crafting a breathtaking portrait of resilience, growth, and self-love.

As you commence your journey to conquer low self-esteem, let forgiveness be your steadfast companion. Embrace it and experience it with joy.

b) Positive affirmations

Remember the negative voice inside you? The one that brings you down? It's time to say "no" to it and replace it with positive affirmations. This might feel challenging initially, but it's a critical step towards improving your self-esteem.

c) Positive relationships

If your low self-esteem has been influenced by negative relationships, it's time to surround yourself with positivity. Build relationships with people who uplift you and believe in you. Let go of any relationship that brings you down. Positive relationships can be a powerful tool for boosting your self-esteem.

d) Assertiveness

Lastly, practice assertiveness. It's about expressing yourself confidently without aggression. Identify situations where you've previously felt insecure and gradually build your confidence.

Learning to improve your self-esteem isn't a one-time thing, it's a journey. By practicing forgiveness, positivity, building meaningful relationships, and assertiveness, you can gradually boost your self-esteem. Don't be discouraged if you don't see immediate results. Remember, it's a process. With time and consistent effort, you can overcome low self-esteem and feel more confident in your own skin.

5. Self-Limiting Beliefs

Do you feel like you are continuously living in a box? Do you feel like your beliefs are limiting your potential? You are not alone. We've all been in situations where we've let our beliefs hinder our progress. But, my friend, it's finally time to shatter those walls and open up to the infinite possibilities within us.

Let's delve into some of the common self-limiting beliefs that you and many others might have encountered:

a) Do you constantly feel like you're not good enough?

This belief might make you question your abilities and potential. It tends to overshadow the greatness in you. However, you should never forget that you are worthy of love, happiness, and achieving your dreams.

b) Have you ever felt like you don't deserve success?

This belief tends to eat away at your self-esteem and makes you feel unworthy of pursuing your dreams. Remember, you deserve all the beautiful moments and rewards that come with your accomplishments.

c) Do you believe that your age is a barrier to success?

This belief often limits opportunities and undervalues your skills and experiences. Let me reassure you, age is just a number. Your experiences and talents hold immense value and wisdom, regardless of your age.

d) Do you tend to underestimate yourself, thinking you're not smart or talented enough?

This belief can deter you from tackling challenges and recognising your potential. Remember, growth and effort are just as important as inherent talents. You are capable of more than you might realise.

e) Do you feel the need to please everyone?

This belief can trap you in a cycle of seeking validation from others, inhibiting you from asserting your needs. It's essential to prioritise your needs and desires. It's okay not to be everything to everyone.

f) Do you think failure implies weakness?

This belief can deter you from taking risks due to the fear of failure. Remember, failure is a stepping stone to growth and success. Embrace the risk, and you might be surprised by the rewards.

g) Are you striving for perfection?

This chase often sets unrealistic standards, causing anxiety, fear of failure, and robbing you of joy. Embrace the beauty of imperfection, perfection is an illusion, and your uniqueness is what makes you shine.

h) Do you believe you are destined to be unhappy?

This belief can trap you in a negative mindset, making it hard to find joy and fulfilment. Remember, you are not destined for anything other than greatness. Embrace positivity and find joy in the little things that make you happy.

i) Do you believe you don't have enough time, money, or resources?

This belief can limit your ability to explore opportunities. However, creativity and resourcefulness can lead you to unexpected opportunities.

Now, let's explore together how to overcome these self-limiting beliefs and begin a beautiful journey of self-discovery and growth.

Are you ready to conquer your self-limiting beliefs?

This liberating journey starts with understanding and compassion for yourself. Let's dive into three powerful steps that will help you break the chains of these beliefs and unleash your boundless potential.

Step 1: Write down your self-limiting beliefs

Have you ever reflected on the self-limiting beliefs that govern your thoughts? Take a moment, grab a journal or open a Notes app on your phone, or even create a document on your computer. Track your negative thoughts for a week or two. I've left some space in this section of the book for you to jot down your thoughts. What patterns are emerging?

Are you noticing beliefs such as "I'm not good enough", "I don't deserve success", or "I'm too old/young to achieve my dreams"? Write these down without judgment, acknowledging their existence in your mind.

____

____

____

____

____

____

____

Step 2: Challenge your beliefs

Now that you have your list, are you ready to challenge these beliefs? It is time to examine them and question their validity. Write down why you think they are incorrect. Dig deeper, scrutinize the evidence that supports them. For instance, if you believe you're not good enough, ask yourself, "What proof do I have that I'm not good enough?" Find reasons why this belief is incorrect. Remember times when you were successful, received praise, or made a positive impact on others. Understand that your worth is not tied to external validation or achievements.

____

____

____

____

____

____

____

Also, identify tangible steps to conquer these beliefs. If you think you don't deserve success, challenge yourself to list your achievements, skills, and qualities. Understand that success comes in various forms and is not restricted to a specific group of people. Embrace self-compassion and remind yourself that you are deserving of achieving your dreams.

Step 3: Practice positive self-talk

Have you ever considered the power of positive self-talk? Catch yourself when you think a limiting thought and replace it with a positive one. For example, instead of thinking "I don't have enough talent", tell yourself "I have unique talents and skills that I can continue to develop". The more you practice, the more it becomes a habit. Positive self-talk can rewire your brain, allowing you to cultivate a more nurturing and supportive mindset.

Celebrate every bit of progress and be patient with yourself in this journey. As you actively challenge and replace self-limiting beliefs with positive affirmations, you'll start to see a transformation within yourself. Surround yourself with a community that uplifts and supports your growth. Remember, you have the power to shape your beliefs and unlock your full potential. Embrace this empowering journey with love and determination, and witness as you tap into the extraordinary potential within you. Believe in yourself. Know that you are destined to break free from the constraints holding you back and embrace a life brimming with purpose and fulfilment.

6. Lack of support

Feeling unsupported in your journey to harness your unique gifts? You may feel that no one understands your aspirations or recognises the value of your skills. Let me assure you though, you are not alone and there are ways to overcome this obstacle.

Firstly, it's crucial to remember that not everyone will comprehend or appreciate your gifts the way you do. People may be biased, have limited perspectives, or simply lack the awareness of your abilities. But, should that discourage you? Absolutely not! Embrace your gifts and trust in their value, even if others may not fully understand them.

So, how can you navigate the lack of support?

Instead of being disheartened, seek out those who inspire you. Surround yourself with a community that understands and appreciates your unique talents. As an aspiring entrepreneur, for instance, you could join networking events or engage in online communities where you can connect with like-minded individuals.

Support can come in many forms and sometimes from unexpected sources. It may not always be available within your immediate circle. Have you considered looking beyond your immediate surroundings? Connect with those who have walked a similar path and can provide invaluable advice. For example, if you're an aspiring writer, you could engage with established authors and learn from their experiences.

Remember, the quality of support is more crucial than the quantity. A small circle of genuine supporters can have a deeper impact on your journey than a large group who may not truly understand your vision. Are you seeking those who believe in you and inspire you to reach new heights?

Professional advice can also be beneficial. Coaches, mentors, and experts in various fields can provide personalised support and help you navigate any challenges you may face. If you're a budding photographer, for instance, investing in a workshop or working with a mentor can help refine your skills.

While external support is essential, have you considered the power of self-confidence and self-validation? Celebrate your achievements and remember your unique strengths. Your journey relies not just on others' validation, but on your unwavering belief in yourself as well.

When faced with a lack of support, remember your gifts are unique and precious. Stand firm in your resolve and trust that the right support will come into your life at the right time. Continue to nurture your gifts with the knowledge that you're destined to make a difference. The world is waiting for you to embrace your gifts, and with self-confidence, genuine relationships, and a supportive community, you're prepared to overcome any obstacle and create a meaningful impact in the world.

7. Comparison and Envy

Have you ever found yourself trapped in the vicious cycle of comparison and envy? It's a common experience. You see someone succeeding in an area where you too possess skills and talents, and suddenly, a wave of envy rushes over you. You begin to question your own abilities, and discouragement sets in. But remember this important fact: your journey is unique and comparing yourself to others only dims your own light.

Let's illustrate this with a real-life scenario. Suppose you're passionate about writing and you happen to meet a best-selling author whose work you deeply admire. It's tempting, isn't it? To compare your work to theirs and wonder why you haven't achieved similar success. But here's what you should remember: every writer's journey is unique. The success of this author doesn't lessen the value of your own work. Your unique voice and storytelling abilities have the power to move people. So, focus on honing your craft and trusting in your own unique perspective.

So, how can you free yourself from the grip of comparison and envy?

The key is to shift from a mindset of competition to one of collaboration. Seek out others who share your interests or passions. If you're an artist, why not join local art communities or groups? Instead of viewing fellow artists as competitors, see them as sources of inspiration and learning. Sharing experiences and ideas will not only enhance your growth, but also build a supportive network for everyone involved.

It's also important to remember that what you see on the surface is often not the full picture. Take social media, for example. It often portrays a polished version of people's lives, hiding their struggles and failures. So, when you catch yourself comparing your journey to someone else's, remember that there's more to their story than what's visible. It's like admiring a stunning beach sunset photo without knowing the storm that came before it.

Self-compassion is another powerful tool to combat comparison and envy. Be gentle with yourself. Recognise that it's natural to have moments of self-doubt or feelings of inadequacy. Treat yourself with the same empathy you'd offer to a good friend in a similar situation. Your worth is not defined by how you measure up to others, but by your unique gifts and talents. Engage in self-care practices that nourish your mind, body, and spirit.

Finally, focus on your own gifts and passions. Redirect your energy from comparison to personal growth. Set goals that align with your passions and take small steps each day towards achieving them. Celebrate your progress and achievements, no matter how small they may seem compared to others. Success is not a race, but a personal journey.

Dear reader, your gifts are extraordinary. They have the potential to inspire, uplift, and create change. Embrace your journey with confidence, compassion, and a commitment to your own growth. Surround yourself with a supportive community, celebrate your uniqueness, and remember that your voice and authentic contributions are needed in the world. By letting go of comparison and envy, you unlock your untapped potential and fully express your gifts in your own unique way.

8. Procrastination

Are you finding yourself constantly putting off tasks for another day? Procrastination is a classic behaviour and an all-too-common obstacle that can stop us from fully harnessing our talents. Procrastination is our tendency to delay or put off tasks, frequently choosing short-term comfort over long-term benefits. It can creep into various areas of our lives, from our artistic pursuits to personal goals. But I want you to remember this – you hold the power to conquer this hurdle and unleash the full might of your talents. Let's dive into strategies to tackle procrastination and adopt a more proactive, empowered stance.

Procrastination often hides behind fleeting moments of leisure or the need to dodge the discomfort of taking action. Consider this scenario: you have a burning passion for writing and dream of authoring a novel. But the sight of a blank page is daunting, and you constantly find yourself delaying the writing process, distracting yourself with other activities instead. I can relate to this because procrastination delayed my progress in writing the book you're reading now. What should have been a few weeks or months turned into seven long years! It's important to remember that underneath the layers of fear and resistance that feed procrastination, lies a stream of untapped potential waiting to be set free.

So, how can you tackle procrastination?

It's essential to start by understanding why you tend to delay tasks. What fears, doubts, or uncertainties are holding you back? Are you afraid of failing or do you worry about criticism? Or is the magnitude of the task simply overwhelming you? By recognising these emotional obstacles, you can face them and shift your perspective. Remember, progress isn't always a straight line. Challenges are a normal part of the journey. Isn't it empowering to know that every small step forward is a victory in itself?

To conquer procrastination, have you tried creating a structured, manageable plan? Break down your goals into smaller, achievable steps and establish a realistic timeline. For instance, if launching your own business is your dream, identify necessary tasks like market research, business plan development or skill acquisition. Doesn't breaking down the process into manageable tasks make it less daunting and easier to start? And don't forget to celebrate every little achievement along the way, as they fuel your motivation and help you push past procrastination.

Accountability can be your secret weapon in the battle against procrastination. Have you considered sharing your goals with a trusted friend, mentor, or accountability partner? Regular check-ins with them about your progress, challenges, and victories can boost your motivation. Isn't it inspiring to know someone is cheering you on and awaiting your updates? Also, consider joining communities of like-minded individuals. Engaging with others who share your aspirations can provide a sense of camaraderie and keep you motivated.

Mindfulness can also be a game-changer in overcoming procrastination. Make it a habit to be present and notice when you're drifting off-course. When you find yourself procrastinating, take a moment and ask yourself: "What am I feeling right now? Why am I resisting?" By recognising your emotions and refocusing, you can consciously decide to act. Why not try mindfulness practices like meditation, deep breathing, or journalling to enhance self-awareness and maintain a clear, focused mind?

Remember to be kind to yourself when faced with procrastination. Setbacks are a natural part of the journey. When you find yourself delaying tasks, instead of criticizing yourself, why not offer understanding and forgiveness? Isn't it comforting to know that every day offers a fresh start? Celebrate your victories, no matter how small, when you overcome procrastination and take action. Fostering self-compassion creates a nurturing environment that allows for growth.

Finally, don't be afraid to silence your inner critic. Remember, your talents are unique and deserve to be shared with the world. By addressing procrastination, you're opening doors to new opportunities and unlocking your true potential. Embrace self-awareness, create a strategic plan, seek accountability, practice mindfulness, and cultivate compassion. By doing so, you'll gradually loosen the grip of procrastination and fully express your talents, making a lasting impact on the world. Believe in yourself, take that first step, and let your unique talents shine for all to see.

ACTION STEPS FOR YOU:

Chapter 4 – Breaking Free: Overcome the Obstacles to Your Gift	
Face your fears	Acknowledge your fears and face them head-on. Remember that fear is a natural part of growth, but it does not define you. Use courage as a tool to overcome fear and unlock the potential of your gift.
Boost your self-confidence	Challenge self-doubt and negative self-talk. Replace them with positive affirmations and a belief in your abilities. Building self-confidence allows you to confidently embrace and share your gift.
Surround Yourself with Positivity	Stay away from negative influences. Instead, surround yourself with people who support and uplift you. Look for a community that celebrates your uniqueness and helps you develop a positive mindset.

Together you can overcome obstacles and thrive.

Chapter 5

The Power Within: Your Gift's Untapped Potential

"A man's gift makes room for him and brings him before the great" - Proverbs 18:16 (ESV)

Have you ever pondered the consequences if the sun simply vanished or if rain ceased to fall for years on end? We depend on these natural phenomena for our survival. Can you imagine the upheaval if they suddenly ceased their roles? A sustained absence of the sun or rain could lead to catastrophic outcomes. This scenario is mirroring distress endured by those who are deprived of your unique gift.

Remember a time when you faced hardships. Perhaps you needed professional help, like a therapist, to navigate the stormy waters. Or maybe it was a very close friend you reached out to. You could have been on a downward spiral without their intervention. Remember that exceptional person who helped you weather the storm? Observing the interaction you had with them, it was clear they were utilising their innate gift. It was their unique talent that made the difference. Have you ever thought about what it would be like if you tapped into your own unique gift in this way? By doing so, you could change lives and make the world a better place.

Take a moment to consider whether any other therapist – or friend – could have been as effective as the one that helped you during your time of need. Of all the professionals or friends available, you were fortunate to find the one that was just right for you. This underpins the importance of utilising your own unique gift. There may be a multitude of people with talents similar to yours – therapists, musicians, artists, writers, and so forth – but none of them can deliver what you can in the way that you do. Your gift is one-of-a-kind and is meant to fulfil a specific need. So why not let it shine so those in need can find their way to you?

You might fear that the world is saturated with people who possess similar gifts. However, understand that your gift is designed to cater to specific individuals who will seek you out when they require it. Never undervalue the influence of your gift. By harnessing it, you have the potential to transform the world for the better.

1. Happiness and Success through Your Gift

Have you ever met someone who's truly in their element, loving what they do and doing it remarkably well? I know an individual who is a pro at housing maintenance, using his creativity not just to fix things but to transform homes into perfect reflections of their inhabitants. Can you visualise the satisfaction he draws from seeing the stunning transformation of a house after he's done with it? His success is no surprise, is it? He is leveraging his natural skills and is thoroughly enjoying it.

Similarly, another acquaintance of mine is a brilliant poet, an eloquent public speaker, and an inspiring teacher. Her words resonate deeply with people, leaving them impacted and eager for more. In fact, I can feel the anticipation when people wait to read her latest work or hear her profound words. She's honed her natural talents to the point where they're not just profitable but deeply gratifying, and the recommendations and recognition she receives are a testament to that.

Now, let's turn the spotlight on you. Does your work bring you joy? Are you harnessing your innate talents to their full potential? Are there any hurdles currently blocking your path to truly embrace what you're naturally good at? Have you, for any reason, concealed your unique gifts?

If you're not doing what you love or if you've been suppressing your gifts and talents, you may be missing out on a fulfilling and joyful life. The secret to unlocking that life? It lies in the effective utilisation of your unique gifts.

2. Creating Space For Your Gift to Shine

Can you picture your unique talent as a golden key? This key isn't just any key – it's the one that unlocks opportunities and leads you to meet inspiring individuals. Isn't it fascinating how a line from an ancient text beautifully puts this concept? It says, **"A person's gift will open doors for them and take them to meet important people."** (Proverbs 18:16). Your gift, your talent, is like the missing piece in a grand jigsaw puzzle that makes the whole image come alive and make sense.

Are you waiting for the perfect moment to showcase your brilliance? Waiting for all the stars to perfectly align? I want to tell you, that perfect moment may never come. Why not start now? Think of your gift as a seed. The earlier you sow it, the sooner it blossoms into something wonderful.

Have you heard of Joseph's story? The biblical story of his life is a perfect example of how a gift can create space for someone. His unique talent for interpreting dreams took him from being a slave to standing beside the king as an advisor. Joseph's journey wasn't easy, but his talent shone even in the toughest of times. So, what's stopping you from letting your talent shine?

Are you afraid that your talent might not be enough? That it won't find its place? But remember, even the smallest spark can light up an entire room. Be like Joseph, let your talent guide you through challenges and bring you amazing experiences.

Let me share a story of my personal experience. I'm a Digital Systems Analyst. Yes, I deal with complex computer systems and problem-solving, which I thoroughly enjoy and excel at. Once, I had the chance to work in Burkina Faso, a country in West Africa. I was worried, but I took this opportunity. Upon my arrival, I was overwhelmed with a sense of accomplishment and joy. I could use my talent to teach and support my colleagues, bridging the gap between digital systems and real-world solutions. Their positive feedback made it all worth it.

Stepping into the space your gift creates could initially feel a bit uncomfortable, but that's where the magic happens. That's where you find your purpose, make a difference, and experience the joy of utilising your unique abilities. So, don't hold back. Let your talent shine, and see how it illuminates not just your life, but also those around you.

Remember, using your talent is not just about achieving things. It's about finding fulfilment, establishing meaningful connections, and making a positive impact. So, when are you going to let your talent shine?

3. Solving Challenges: See Your Gift as a Solution

Do you know someone who has the uncanny ability to light up a room with their smile? Someone who creates an atmosphere of laughter and happiness, instantly lifting the spirits of those around them? Now, imagine if they decided to keep this infectious positivity to themselves. Wouldn't that cast a shadow on those moments that could have been filled with joy and connection? This is exactly how it is with your unique gift – it holds the potential to be a solution to someone's problem.

Have you ever considered the impact you could make by not sharing your gift? When you decide to withhold it, you might be preventing someone from finding the solution they desperately need. Your gift – whether it's a kind word, a helping hand, or a creative idea, can make a world of difference. So, do you want to be a source of joy for someone or do you want to contribute to their problems?

Understand this – your gift is not just about you. It's about the positive effect you can have on others. When you muster the courage to share your gift, you become a problem solver.

Let me share a personal story. Once, when I was trying to learn new skills while working full time, I considered using my fluency in French and English for written translation or interpretation. But my love for spoken communication led me to community interpreting and bilingual advocacy. Little did I know that this decision would open doors to a life-altering opportunity.

When Haiti was hit by a devastating earthquake in 2010, I volunteered to help. After landing there, I quickly realised there was a significant language barrier. Being the only one fluent in both English and French – and basic Haitian creole

–, I became the crucial link between the English-speaking team and the local community, solving a pressing communication problem.

Isn't it fascinating how using our gifts can lead to grander things? It's a ripple effect – you share your gift and it triggers a chain reaction of positivity. It's not just about helping others; it's about creating a cycle of goodness that comes back to enrich your life as well.

Let me share another example of the incredible impact of using your gifts. A woman I know has an incredible talent for connecting with people. She creates an environment of understanding and comfort wherever she goes. But imagine if she had never acknowledged this gift.

She was once in a park, deep in conversation with a friend, when she noticed a distressed woman nearby. Instead of ignoring the woman and continuing her conversation, she approached her, offered a comforting smile and asked if everything was okay. It turned out the woman was overwhelmed with work-related problems. She didn't provide immediate solutions or advice. She simply listened, empathised, and understood. And that made all the difference. By the end of their conversation, the woman was relieved and thankful for her willingness to listen and understand.

Isn't that a testament to the transformative power of utilising your gift to solve problems? My friend's gift of connection had turned a moment of distress into one of hope. You don't have to be an expert or have all the answers – your genuine presence can be a game changer. Your gift, no matter how simple, can have a profound impact on people's lives.

So why hide your gift or underestimate its potential? It has the power to change circumstances, uplift spirits, and inspire change. Embrace it, share it, and observe as you become a source of solutions in a world that needs them. Remember, your gift is your solution, and the world is waiting for it.

4. Your Gift Makes You Fruitful and Productive

My hope is that, by now, you realise the magnificent power you possess. Inside you lies a unique gift, a special talent that can not only bring joy to your life but also make a significant difference in the world. This isn't dictated by your beliefs or background, but by your own unique capabilities.

Imagine a tree, bountiful with succulent fruits. Your gifts are much like these fruits, they represent goodness, happiness, and the potential to enact change. How does it feel when you tap into your gifts? Doesn't it bring a sense of fulfilment and joy?

Consider the story of Winnie, an ordinary person just like you and me, yet with an extraordinary ability to listen. Her keen sense of understanding others makes her friends feel cherished and connected. Her story is a testament to the fact that utilising your gifts can enrich not only your life but also those around you.

Or take the example of Julia's friends. They used their unique talents in cooking, photography, and event planning to uplift their community. Doesn't their story illustrate how our skills can foster positive change and benefit others?

But recognising your talents is just the beginning. It's akin to nurturing a tree for it to bear fruit. You need to work on honing your special gifts to unleash their true potential.

True, the journey to developing your gifts may be filled with uncertainties and challenges, but each step is an opportunity for growth. How does it feel knowing that by embracing and practicing your gifts, you're not only improving your own life but also positively impacting those around you?

Regardless of your beliefs, the significance of nurturing your talents remains the same. Your abilities are tools that can bring happiness, purpose, and positive changes to your life and others. So, are you ready to embark on this journey?

Let's work together to discover and enhance your unique abilities. By putting them into practice, we can create a meaningful and impactful life. After all, the world is eager to witness the incredible things you can do with your gifts.

Producing Good Fruits

Have you ever thought about how you can use your unique skills and talents for the greater good? Regardless of whether you're religious or not, the concept of producing good fruits is something we can all stand behind. It's all about using your abilities to create positive change in our world.

Take, for example, Michelle Obama, who is a great source of inspiration when it comes to this principle. Can you imagine what it's like to use your skills of communication, empathy, and leadership to champion significant causes like education, health, and equality? Just like her, you, too, can make a lasting impact on people's lives, empowering them to believe in their potential and strive for a better future.

Do you believe that your actions should benefit others and contribute to society's well-being? If so, producing good fruits is a principle you're already familiar with. It simply emphasises that your skills should be used in a manner that uplifts, inspires, and brings about positive change.

But what about the opposite? Producing bad fruits means using your skills in a destructive or negative manner. It could mean using your talents to manipulate or deceive others, spreading negativity, or causing harm. If we use our skills to tear others down or promote injustice, in effect we are adding to the cycle of negativity and suffering.

Therefore, isn't it crucial to be conscious of how our actions impact others and the world around us? Producing good fruits is a deliberate choice to use our skills in ways that foster love, compassion, understanding, and positive change. By aligning our intentions and actions with values such as kindness, integrity, and respect, I believe we could create a ripple effect of positivity.

Remember, we all have the power to make choices that lead to positive outcomes. No matter how influential or recognised we are, we can make a meaningful impact by using our talents for good. Whether it's through small acts of kindness, service, or standing up for what's right, we can contribute to a more compassionate and just world.

Think about where you come from and the significance of your thoughts and intentions in shaping your actions. Isn’t it vital to nurture a mindset rooted in kindness, integrity, and a genuine desire to help others? By doing so, we can ensure that our talents are used in ways that bring about positive outcomes.

Let's seize the opportunity to produce good fruits, following in the footsteps of inspiring leaders like Michelle Obama, the former First Lady of the United States of America, as previously mentioned. Other remarkable leaders such as Malala Yousafzai, a global advocate for girls' education and the youngest Nobel Prize laureate, Jacinda Ardern, the Prime Minister of New Zealand who has demonstrated exceptional leadership in times of crisis, and Oprah Winfrey, a media mogul and philanthropist who has used her platform to inspire and empower millions around the world. They are all remarkable women who have used their platforms to inspire and empower others. So, are you ready to join them in making a difference?

Boosting Your Productivity

You possess unique gifts and talents, which are powerful engines driving your productivity and creating positive change in the world. Have you ever considered how your unique abilities contribute to your productivity and success? Let's explore this together, drawing inspiration from real-life examples.

Expertise that shines: Your gifts and talents equip you with specialized knowledge and skills. Have you ever thought about how these can help you excel in your field and achieve extraordinary results? For instance, if you're naturally good at problem-solving and have analytical thinking skills, you could become an excellent strategist. How does this increase your productivity? It enables you to find creative solutions and achieve your goals more effectively.

Inspiring creativity: Do you know that your gifts and talents can ignite your creativity and foster innovation? They empower you to approach tasks from fresh perspectives, opening up new possibilities. Picture yourself as a graphic designer with a knack for visual communication and a talent for combining colours and typography. Your creative flair could enable you to produce stunning designs that captivate audiences and elevate brands.

Empowering others: Did you know your gifts and talents can inspire and uplift those around you? Sharing your unique abilities can aid others in realising their potential and flourishing. Consider a mentor, their ability to guide and listen attentively could help others overcome challenges, chase their dreams, and achieve personal and professional growth.

Resilience in the face of challenges: Your talents and gifts provide resilience in the face of challenges. They equip you with the internal resources to persist when things get tough. Think about a professional athlete who has athletic prowess and discipline. Their unwavering dedication allows them to push beyond their limits and achieve incredible feats.

Creating connections: Your gifts and talents can also create connections. They foster collaboration and teamwork, enabling you to work together with others to achieve shared goals. Picture an entrepreneur with a talent for networking and relationship building. Their ability to connect people drives productivity by harnessing collective strengths and resources.

Let's look at real-world examples like that of Michelle Bachelet, former President of Chile and a renowned human rights advocate. Bachelet used her gifts of compassion, diplomacy and strategic thinking to drive productivity and create positive change in Chile. How did her gifts benefit society? They led to the implementation of progressive policies that reduced poverty, improved health care, and advanced gender equality. Through embracing her unique abilities, Bachelet had a profound impact on countless lives. Her commitment to social justice and inclusivity has earned her international acclaim. She's a perfect example of how using our gifts can boost productivity and contribute to a more equitable and prosperous society.

To sum up, your gifts and talents have immense potential to increase productivity and create a meaningful impact. Embrace and nurture these unique abilities. They can help you excel, spark creativity, empower others, cultivate resilience, and build strong connections. Trust in your gifts, make the most of them, and watch your productivity soar while positively impacting the lives of others.

Ultimately, it is important to recognise that, as women, we make a difference in our everyday life. Have you ever stopped to consider that you, yes you, are a leader in your own right? Regardless of how wide your sphere of influence is, or how much recognition you garner, your personal leadership matters. The stories of prominent female leaders inspire us, but remember, leadership isn't confined to the limelight.

Are you a new mom? Have you just launched a business? Maybe, you're an individual who's searching for a purpose? Or perhaps, you're a single or retired woman? Regardless of where you stand, you have the power to make a difference in your unique way.

Think about it. Each decision you make, every action you take, and the contributions you offer can inspire and positively impact those around you. Isn't it amazing to think that you can influence those in your family, community, or workplace?

Imagine leaving a legacy of compassion, empowerment, and positive change. It could be through art, mentorship, innovation, leadership, community involvement, advocacy, caregiving, or any other form of contribution. Aren't we all capable of using our talents and skills to create a better world?

Yes, you have the power, the ability to inspire and make a difference. The question is: are you ready to step up and embrace your leadership potential?

5. Personal Fulfilment: The Joy of Living Your Gift

Imagine the feeling of waking up each morning, your heart filled with purpose and excitement. Can you envision that moment, that spark of joy as you realise you're about to spend your day doing something that deeply resonates with your soul? That's the power of living your gift. When you tap into your unique abilities, your self-esteem blossoms, life becomes more enriching, and personal fulfilment takes on a whole new meaning.

You see, the journey towards personal fulfilment begins by acknowledging the intrinsic worth of your gift. It's not merely about what you're capable of doing; it's about who you are at your core. Your gift is like a treasure hidden deep within you, waiting to be unearthed and shared with the world. When you tap into this potential, you start seeing a different reflection in the mirror. Your confidence escalates as you realise there's something extraordinary about you, something that distinguishes you from others.

Let's take a moment to explore an inspiring story that beautifully showcases the power of harnessing your gift for personal fulfilment. Picture Jane, a busy mother of three who always had a knack for organising. Friends and family have always admired her ability to flawlessly host gatherings, turning even the simplest of events into memorable experiences. Jane's gift for creating warm and inviting environments is undeniable.

One day, a close friend, feeling overwhelmed about hosting a baby shower, confided in Jane. Without a second thought, Jane offered to help. She transformed the event into a stunning, joy-filled celebration that left everyone astounded. Word of her talent spread, and Jane found herself being asked to help with various community events.

Initially, Jane hesitated. She pondered whether she had the time or expertise for these added responsibilities. But then, she realised her gift could bring joy, relief, and ease to others during their special moments. Embracing her gift, she turned her passion for event planning into a small business.

As Jane poured her heart into her new venture, she discovered that her gift not only brought happiness to others but also filled her with a profound sense of fulfilment. Through her creative touch, Jane managed to turn ordinary gatherings into extraordinary experiences, leaving her clients overjoyed and grateful.

I actually had a very similar experience of having a wonderful and gifted friend organise what was meant to be a short and simple wedding ceremony into a memorable and sumptuous wedding celebration. She planned and coordinated my wedding in just a few weeks. And was it a success? Absolutely it was! My husband and I are so grateful for it. My friend had just turned her love for event planning into a business. And it is thriving.

Now, think of your gift. Can you see the impact it could have on your life and the lives of those around you? Living your gift also brings a deep sense of satisfaction. Remember the times when you've achieved something meaningful? That feeling of satisfaction is amplified when your efforts align with your natural talents. You start to experience fulfilment that transcends external validation. It's a contentment that originates from within, a validation of your unique essence.

Let's consider Amber, who always loved art but never pursued it seriously due to societal pressures. Eventually, she could no longer suppress her creative urge and started devoting time to her artwork. As she allowed her gift to blossom, Amber found herself in a state of flow whenever she painted. The satisfaction she derived from creating art was unlike anything she had experienced before.

Living your gift isn't about seeking perfection; it's about embracing authenticity. When you use your gift, you're being your true self, and that authenticity shines through in everything you do. It resonates with others, creating deeper connections and relationships.

Ultimately, living your gift is a transformative experience. When you align your actions with your natural abilities, your self-esteem flourishes, and your days become filled with purpose and satisfaction. Can you picture that? Through examples like Jane and Amber, it's clear that personal fulfilment is within reach when you embrace the potential of your gift and share it with the world.

Your gift isn't just a skill; it's an integral part of who you are. Can you feel the excitement of embarking on a journey towards a more empowered and fulfilling life when you let it shine?

As we come to the end of this section, consider this; your gifts and talents have incredible potential. They can supercharge your productivity and you can create a genuine impact. See yourself nurturing these unique abilities to excel in your field, generate fresh ideas, inspire others, overcome challenges, and forge strong connections.

But let's not lose sight of the fact that we're all leaders in our own unique ways. Whether you're a new mom, starting a business, walking the path alone, retired, or on a hunt for your purpose, you can lead and make a difference.

So, as we prepare to delve deeper into how to unlock your gift and how you can make a difference in the world, think about this: leadership is not reserved for the famous. We all have power within us. Isn’t that a beautiful thought?

ACTION STEPS FOR YOU:

Chapter 5 - The Power Within: Your Gift's Untapped Potential	
Embrace Happiness and Success	Understand that using your gift not only brings joy to others, but also to yourself. It also leads to success in various aspects of life. Embrace the positive impact, happiness and fulfilment that comes from sharing your unique abilities.
Create Opportunities	Realise that your gift opens doors for you. As you use it, you will discover new avenues and opportunities to make a difference and achieve your goals. Keep an open mind and seize these opportunities.
Be a problem solver	Recognise that your gift is a solution to someone's problem. Whether big or small, your unique abilities can positively impact the lives of others. Embrace the value your gift adds to the world.

Chapter 6

Gift Unlocked: Make Your Mark on the World

"The meaning of life is to find your gift. The purpose of life is to give it away." - Pablo Picasso

Wow! You've made it this far, clearly indicating your readiness to harness your unique gift. Now, it's time to delve deeper into the powerful ways you can utilise this gift to positively impact others and the world. Remember, your gift isn't just for your personal satisfaction. It's a mighty tool that can touch lives and trigger lasting transformation. In this chapter, I will share real-life examples of women who have used their gift to make their mark on the world. Their stories will undoubtedly inspire you. Are you ready to explore the extraordinary opportunities that await?

1. Embrace Your Purpose

Understanding your purpose is instrumental in unlocking your gift's full potential. It's about aligning your natural talents with a profound sense of purpose and impact. Have you pondered what sparks passion within you? The answers can provide precious insights into where your gift can truly flourish. And having read the previous chapters, by now I would hope you were able to identify some specific causes or aspects of life that ignite a fire within you. Could it be the power of storytelling that fascinates you, allowing you to inspire others through art? Or maybe you have a natural talent for empathy, enabling you to ease people's suffering and provide comfort in hard times. Or perhaps it's your analytical mind that thrives on cracking complex problems, enabling you to find innovative solutions that benefit society.

To highlight the power of aligning your gift with your purpose, let's explore some real-life examples.

Sarah, the artist

Consider Sarah, an incredibly talented painter who finds peace and joy in expressing her emotions through vibrant colours and intricate brushstrokes. Upon reflection, Sarah realises she has a desire to use her gift to raise awareness about mental health. She creates a series of paintings that illustrate the emotional journey of those grappling with mental health issues. Through her art, Sarah not only encourages others to talk about their struggles but also raises funds for organisations providing mental health support.

Danielle, the empath

Next, let's think about Danielle, a naturally empathetic individual with a talent for listening and understanding others. Danielle acknowledges a deep yearning to support people dealing with grief and loss. She channels her gift by becoming a grief counsellor, providing a compassionate ear, and guiding others through their healing journeys. Danielle's empathetic nature becomes a beacon of hope for those navigating the depths of grief, helping them find strength and resilience in their darkest moments.

Maya, the innovator

Finally, let's meet Maya, an exceptional problem solver with an analytical mind. Maya is passionate about environmental sustainability and recognises her purpose lies in finding innovative solutions to combat climate change. She applies her gift to develop sustainable technologies, collaborating with scientists and engineers to create renewable energy sources and reduce carbon emissions. Maya's contributions significantly impact the environment, revolutionising the way we generate and consume energy and paving the path for a greener future.

Imagine if you, like Sarah, Danielle, and Maya, could connect your gift with a purpose that resonates deeply with your values. Embracing your purpose infuses your gift with intention and direction, steering it towards serving others and making a positive difference. Remember, your purpose may evolve as you grow and gain new experiences. Remain open to the possibilities and tune into your heart's whispers as you embark on this fascinating journey.

As you embrace your purpose, believe in the power of your gift and the profound effect it can have on those around you. Whether you choose to inspire, heal, innovate, or spread joy, the world is eager to receive the unique contribution only you can make. Embrace your purpose with bravery, compassion, and unwavering belief in your ability to create a better world through your gift. Your journey towards making a lasting impact starts now.

2. Identify Who Can Benefit From Your Gift

Are you ready to discover who can truly benefit from your unique gift? It's an essential journey to undertake, as it directs your efforts to have the most profound impact and create positive changes in the lives around you. By knowing your audience, you can focus your unique skills and talents on those who will gain the most from your light. Let's dive into this exploration together.

Think for a moment, who are the people that could be enriched by your knowledge, creativity, or unique viewpoint? Is there a specific group of individuals that resonate with your compassionate soul, a group that you feel a strong urge to help and elevate? Let your heart guide you and listen to its quiet hints of connection and resonance.

Emily, the musician

Take Emily, for example. She is a gifted musician with a knack for teaching. As she reflects on who can benefit from her talents, she connects with her deep bond with children. She realises she can use her musical prowess to inspire young minds, fostering a love for music and creativity. Emily then begins to offer music lessons to children in her community, creating a safe space for them to explore their musical talents. Her commitment not only helps children develop musically, but she also boosts their self-confidence and ignites a lifelong love for the arts.

Katie, the befriender

Now, think about Katie, a kind-hearted individual with a natural talent for offering companionship. Katie realises the significant change she can make in the lives of the elderly as she reflects on who can benefit from her gift. She knows that many older adults experience loneliness and isolation, yearning for meaningful connections. Inspired by her grandmother's stories and her desire to make a difference, Katie decides to volunteer at a local senior centre. She brings comfort and joy to the elderly residents through her regular visits, engaging conversations, and attentive listening. Katie's companionship alleviates their loneliness and contributes to their overall mental health, reminding them that they are loved and valued.

Helen, the entrepreneur

Finally, picture Helen, a determined entrepreneur who has successfully juggled new motherhood while running her own business. When she considers who can benefit from her experiences, she identifies other new mothers aspiring to start or grow their businesses. Helen understands the unique challenges of balancing motherhood and entrepreneurship. Motivated by her own journey and the desire to foster a supportive community, Helen initiates a mentorship program tailored for new mothers in business. She shares her insights and practical strategies, helping them overcome obstacles, achieve work-life balance, and thrive in both roles. Helen's mentorship empowers new mothers to pursue their passions, create successful businesses, and attain financial independence. Through her guidance and support, these women gain the tools and confidence they need to realise their entrepreneurial dreams while embracing the beautiful journey of motherhood.

So, who can benefit from your unique gift? As you reflect on this, remember Emily, Katie, and Helen. Can you see yourself in any of these examples? They identified their audience and harnessed their gifts, creating meaningful change in their communities. You too, can make a difference with your extraordinary gift.

Have you identified the unique gift that you can offer to the world? Who do you believe can benefit the most from your special abilities? Is it children, the elderly, or perhaps those struggling with mental health challenges? Whoever they may be, your unique skills have the potential to touch hearts, uplift souls and spark transformative change.

As you start this meaningful journey of finding your recipients, trust your instincts and let your compassionate heart lead the way. Remain open to new ways your gift can serve others and make a difference. Opportunities may present themselves in ways you never expected. By focusing your efforts on those who need it most, you can magnify the positive impact you bring into the world.

Your gift is a beacon of hope and inspiration, and by sharing it with the right people, you create a ripple effect that reaches far beyond your immediate surroundings.

Remember, there are countless individuals in this world who are longing for what you have to offer. Can you see the beautiful diversity of those who can benefit from your gift? Let your compassionate spirit lead you towards making a lasting impact. The world eagerly awaits your unique contribution. You are valued and needed.

How does it feel to think of sharing your gift with those who will treasure it the most? Together, we can brighten lives and create a world where compassion and light reign supreme.

3. Seek Opportunities To Share Your Unique Gift

As we continue on this transformative journey of embracing our purpose and understanding who can benefit from our extraordinary gifts, let’s open a new chapter. Ready to take your unique gifts to the next level? Now is the time to embrace the opportunities waiting for you, both in your local community and in the digital sphere. Let's begin this exciting journey of making a significant difference in the lives of others.

First, take a close look at your own neighbourhood or city. Can you spot local organisations or groups that align with your values and passions? Perhaps there's a charity or volunteer program that would greatly benefit from your unique skills, creativity, or compassionate nature. How would it feel to apply your gifts to causes that deeply resonate with you?

But let's not forget about the limitless potential of the digital world. In today's tech-savvy era, your unique gifts have the power to touch lives across the globe, breaking down geographical barriers. Have you thought about exploring online platforms, forums, or social media communities where you can share your talents and experiences? Maybe there's a blog where you can write about your expertise, a podcast where you can share your stories, or a YouTube channel where you can inspire and educate others. By utilising the digital platform, you're afforded the chance to connect with individuals who can truly benefit from your gifts, no matter where they are in the world. Imagine the joy of knowing your voice and presence can offer comfort and inspiration to those seeking guidance or feeling alone on their journey.

Let's delve into a few inspiring stories to truly bring the power of your unique gifts to life, shall we?

Rachel, the teacher

Have you ever met someone like Rachel? She's a gifted writer with an unshakeable love for education. One day, Rachel stumbles upon a literacy program in her local community aimed at improving children's reading skills. Spotting a perfect match between her talent and this cause, she steps forward to volunteer as a writing tutor. Can you imagine the joy she gets from using her words to ignite creativity, enhance language skills, and foster a lifelong love for reading and writing in these children? Through her local involvement, she experiences first-hand the transformative power of her gift. Are you ready to nurture the next generation with your unique talents?

Sophia, the chef

Now, let me introduce you to Sophia. She's a talented chef with a profound passion for feeding both the body and the soul. Sophia firmly believes in the right of every person to enjoy wholesome, delicious meals, no matter their circumstances. Does this resonate with you? Driven by her beliefs, she finds a way to make a difference by volunteering at a local community kitchen. Her culinary skills become much more than a means to provide food; they create a warm, inviting space where people can connect and find a sense of belonging. Can you see how your passion can serve as a powerful force for positive change?

Lily, the public speaker

Lastly, let's meet Lily, a naturally inspiring public speaker. She understands the struggles faced by young women without access to education and empowerment. Do you feel called to empower others? Lily does. She uses her gift to mentor underprivileged girls in her community, organising workshops, and speaking at events. Her gift of public speaking empowers these young women, fostering confidence and a sense of limitless possibilities. Can you imagine using your gift to pave the way for a generation of strong leaders?

These stories are just a taste of the countless possibilities that await you. The key? Listen to your heart and embrace the opportunities that align with your calling. The world is waiting for your gift. As you find ways to share it, you'll not only transform others' lives but also experience personal growth and a profound sense of purpose. My hope is that you keep your determination unwavering and let your gift shine brightly, touch hearts, empower souls, and leave a lasting mark on the world. Have confidence and believe in yourself. Opportunities are there if you grab them.

4. Practice Empathy and Compassion

How about stepping into the shoes of someone else for a moment? Imagine the world from their perspective, feel their struggles, and share their dreams. As you use your unique talents to make a difference, are you truly understanding their needs? Are you hearing their tales with genuine interest, allowing their narratives to unfold naturally? By embracing empathy, you are gaining valuable insights into their lives and emotions. This understanding enables you to shape your unique abilities to their specific situations.

Consider adopting the role of a reliable guide, while maintaining a respectful and professional demeanour. Empathy and compassion are your guiding lights on this journey. Does this approach sound like something you could integrate into your journey of making a difference?

Ava, the florist

Imagine you are Ava, a gifted florist. You use your talents to create stunning floral arrangements, don't you? You practice empathy by understanding the emotions connected with different flowers and tailoring your designs to reflect your clients' unique preferences and needs, right? By actively listening to their stories and wishes, you create floral masterpieces that encapsulate their special moments. Do you see how your compassionate approach resonates with your clients?

Maureen, the singer-songwriter

Or perhaps you're more like Maureen, a gifted singer-songwriter, whose music heals and uplifts others. You embed hope and resilience in your lyrics and melodies, don't you? You connect with your audience, engage in conversations and genuinely listen to their stories, right? Through your heartfelt performances, you create a compassionate and understanding atmosphere, reminding your listeners that they are not alone in their struggles. Can you see how your gift of music becomes a beacon of light?

Jennifer, the photographer

Maybe you're more like Jennifer, a talented photographer who captures the essence of people's stories. You approach each photography session with empathy and compassion. You listen to their personal narratives, learning about their triumphs, struggles, and aspirations, right? Through this deep understanding, your photographs not only showcase their physical beauty but also reflect their inner strength and resilience. Can you see how your empathetic approach allows your subjects to feel seen and heard?

Remember, your gift can become a catalyst for positive change and healing. Whether it's through artistic expression, your ability to listen and provide guidance, or your problem-solving talent, your actions can be guided by a desire to make a positive impact. As you interact with others, do you take the time to understand their unique circumstances? By showing empathy, you can help them unlock their potential. Your gift can bring light into their lives, offering solace, inspiration, and hope.

As you engage with others, remember that each person's journey is unique. Approach them with an open heart, free from judgment. Through your empathetic and compassionate approach, can you see how you can forge deep connections and create meaningful change?

By embracing empathy and compassion, you are not only enriching others' lives but also nurturing your own growth. Through your gift, you can touch hearts, inspire change, and create a more compassionate world. So, dear friend, let your kindness shine. Practice empathy and compassion as you share your unique abilities. Together, let's create a world filled with empathy, kindness, and lasting connections.

5. Seek Collaboration and Support

You're one in a million, with a gift that's truly exceptional! But have you ever thought about the fact that no one accomplishes greatness alone? As you begin your journey of using your unique gift for good, why not reach out to like-minded individuals and groups?

Have you considered looking for partners who share your vision and values? Those who align with your vision and values can help increase your impact and join you in this force for good.

Have you ever thought about the power of collaboration and the wonders it brings? Collaboration amplifies the reach and effectiveness of your giving, allowing you to create positive change on a bigger scale. Remember, your extraordinary gift isn't meant to exist in isolation. So, why not seek support and collaboration to make a bigger difference? Let's consider a few examples.

Mia, the actress

Imagine Mia, an accomplished actress who has the knack for bringing people together in laughter. Don't you agree that her joining a female-led theatre group that promotes diverse narratives and empowering stories, amplifies her talent and reaches more people? Can you see how they work together to challenge societal norms and encourage inclusivity?

Alice, the graphic designer

Similarly, picture Alice, a skilled graphic designer who uses her talent to create impactful visual campaigns. Can you envision her working with a group of female photographers and writers, all sharing a common dedication to advocating for women's rights? Together, they create a powerful visual narrative that challenges stereotypes and ignites conversations about equality. Isn't it impressive how Alice and her associates leverage their individual gifts and how they create collective efforts that resonates with audiences worldwide?

Sandra, the educator

Likewise, visualise Sandra, a dedicated educator passionate about inspiring young minds. As she strives to create transformative change, can you see how her collaboration with a women-led nonprofit that aligns with her mission amplifies her impact in educational empowerment? Together, they create workshops and mentorship programs that help disadvantaged girls. Can you see the ripple effect of empowering future female leaders?

Do you see the power of collaboration? By working with others who share your vision and values, you can create an impactful synergy that fosters positive change on a larger scale. Just imagine the potential for growth, learning, and inspiration that collaboration can offer.

Are you hesitant to ask for help? Remember, seeking mentorship or guidance from those who've walked your path is not a sign of weakness but a testament to your strength and willingness to learn. Can you see the value in surrounding yourself with a supportive network of individuals committed to your success?

As you embark on your collaborative path, be open to different perspectives and ideas. Can you appreciate the diversity of ideas and talents that others bring to the table? By harnessing the power of collective creativity and common purpose, you can achieve extraordinary results and create a legacy that goes beyond what you could accomplish alone.

So, seek collaboration and support throughout your journey. Can you feel the power of collective action, and recognise that together we can accomplish so much more than we ever could as individuals? Can you imagine your gift mingling with the gifts of others, creating a symphony of positive change that echoes across the globe? With collaboration, support, and compassion, can you see the lasting impact you can make? This is your chance to leave a legacy of hope, empowerment, and love.

6. Start Small, Dream Big

Do you dream of making a significant difference, dear friend? Remember, you don't always need grand actions or monumental achievements to use your unique gifts. Quite the contrary, it's the small gestures, the little acts of kindness and empathy, that often have the most profound impact.

So, where do you start? How about right here, right now, in your everyday life? There are countless opportunities around you, seemingly insignificant, where you could make a difference. Can you see them? Just say YES when the occasion arises.

Remember, starting small doesn't mean dreaming small. The ripples you create today, no matter how tiny, have the potential to transform lives. You have the power, so why not start today?

Audrey, the storyteller

Have you ever heard of Audrey, the gifted writer? She's someone who's just like you, full of dreams and aspirations. Her goal? To touch the hearts of many through a bestselling novel. But you see, she started small, by sharing her creative stories with her close friends. Now, imagine being one of those friends, huddled in a cosy room, listening to her bring characters to life. Would you not feel inspired? Would her stories not stir up emotions and make you reflect on your own life experiences? Through her small-scale storytelling sessions, Audrey plants seeds of imagination and empathy that can grow and spread far beyond her immediate circle. Her humble beginnings serve as a reminder that you too can inspire those around you through your actions, no matter how small they may seem.

Lauren, the mindset coach

Have you also met Lauren, the mindset coach? She's someone who's passionate about empowering others, just like you may be. Her ultimate dream is to make a global impact but she started by extending her support to her friends. What if you were part of her mindset workshops or individual coaching sessions? Can you imagine the difference it would make to overcome self-limiting beliefs and foster a positive mindset? Lauren's small-scale efforts, just like yours, can have a ripple effect, empowering others to be their best selves.

Priya, the gardener

And then there's Priya, the dedicated gardener, who dreams of creating a botanical paradise. Her starting point? A small community garden in her neighbourhood. Picture yourself walking through the vibrant plants, learning about gardening, and reconnecting with nature. Wouldn't it instil a sense of community pride and appreciation for the environment? Priya's small acts of care demonstrate the potential of your own small actions to inspire others.

Now, remember this, the significance of your actions isn't always about their size or scale. It's about the genuine care and love you put into them. Can you see ways in your everyday life where you can make a positive impact, no matter how small? Why not brighten someone's day with a warm smile or lend a hand to a stranger? Or perhaps you could offer your expertise to someone in need. These simple acts of kindness can create a ripple effect of positivity and compassion.

By taking small steps and focusing on the present, you can build a solid foundation of care, one act at a time. Can you see every interaction as an opportunity to touch someone's life? Your small acts of generosity can add up, leaving a lasting legacy of love and empowerment.

So, dream big, aspire to create transformative change, but remember it starts with the small steps you take today. Can you feel the power of your giving in the moment, knowing that every act of kindness can change the world, one person at a time? Your gift is a beacon of light, hope, and comfort to those who need it most. Can you trust in the profound impact of your small actions and let them inspire you to keep dreaming big?

Together, let's start small and dream big. Let's create a tapestry of love and transformation across the world through our collective acts of kindness and compassion. Can you embrace the magic of the present moment? It holds the power to shape a better future for all.

7. Embrace Continuous Growth

Are you ready to embark on an extraordinary journey, using your unique gifts to enrich the lives of others? It's crucial to remember that growth is a never-ending process. There's always room for improvement, for expansion. Stay open and receptive to learning, feedback, and new experiences as these are the things that can truly deepen your understanding of your gift and its potential impact. Can you see the value in seeking out mentors, role models who have been on the same path you are on?

As your mindset coach, I can't emphasise enough how vital it is to welcome continuous growth. This journey of using your gift to serve others is not a one-time event, but a journey of constant learning, evolving, and growing. Are you ready to embrace this growth and make a positive difference in your life and the lives of others?

Connie, the life coach

Imagine yourself in the shoes of Connie, a brilliant life coach who is passionate about empowering individuals to live their best lives. While she has already made a significant impact through her coaching, Connie is deeply committed to her growth, always seeking out new coaching techniques and engaging in professional development. She knows that being a coach involves being coached too. She seeks guidance from experienced coaches who can provide fresh perspectives, challenge her assumptions, and support her in her own personal and professional development. Do you share Connie's belief in the power of mentorship? Can you see how her commitment to continuous growth and her openness to being coached deepens her understanding and enhances her coaching skills?

Tatiana, the scientist

Or perhaps you identify more with Tatiana, a dedicated scientist. Despite her impressive academic background, she never stops learning, continually pushing the boundaries of scientific exploration. She attends conferences, engages in research collaborations, and participates in professional development programs. Through these experiences, she learns about cutting-edge research, connects with experts in her field, and expands her knowledge base. By embracing continuous growth, Tatiana pushes the boundaries of scientific exploration, discovering new ideas and advances that have the potential to revolutionise medicine and improve health outcomes. Do you also see the value in staying updated with the latest advancements in your field?

Life isn't without challenges, is it? But in these challenges lie tremendous opportunities for personal and professional growth. Do you agree? Each hurdle you encounter is an opportunity to expand your horizons, go beyond your comfort zone, and explore new facets of your skills. Embrace the unknown with courage and curiosity, knowing that every experience, whether successful or challenging, contributes to your growth.

Pam, the software developer

But let's not forget about Pam, a gifted software developer. When faced with a complex programming problem, she doesn't shy away from the challenge. Instead of being overwhelmed, she sees it as a learning opportunity. Can you approach your challenges in the same way? By rising to the occasion and embracing continuous growth, Pam became a more versatile and skilled developer, creating software solutions that positively widen her impact. Can you see how embracing challenges can turn you into a better version of yourself?

Remember, every step of your journey is an opportunity for growth. Are you ready to embrace this process with an open heart and a curious mind? Are you willing to seek knowledge, feedback, and experiences that will help you refine your skills and expand your impact?

Keep embracing growth in your journey. Are you open to learning from mentors and facing challenges with resilience and determination? Your commitment to growth will elevate your contributions, expand your impact, and leave a lasting mark on the world. Do you trust in your ability to grow and make a difference?

Your journey of using your skills to serve others is one of constant growth and learning. Can you see the value in this journey? Do you believe in your potential and trust that you can overcome any challenge that comes your way? As you nurture your skills with continuous growth, they will flourish and impact the lives of those around you in profound ways.

Always remember, you are capable of greatness! Are you ready to embrace continuous growth and see your skills expand and touch the lives of many? Embrace every opportunity for learning and never stop challenging yourself to reach new heights. Your journey is filled with infinite possibilities. Embrace them, learn from them, and let them shape you into the exceptional person you are destined to become.

8. Stay Committed and Resilient

Let's be honest, unlocking the full potential of your unique gift isn't always going be a smooth journey. Challenges and setbacks are inevitable, but it's during these very moments that your dedication and tenacity are truly tested. Remember, your commitment and resilience are what will see you through.

Can you recall the reason why you embarked on this path in the first place? What was that spark of inspiration, that positive change you envisioned creating with your gift? And let's not forget the impact you dreamed of making in the lives of others.

I encourage you to never lose sight of these initial motivations and aspirations. Stay connected to them, for they will serve as your compass in times of doubt and uncertainty. Are you ready to stay committed and resilient in your pursuit?

Elizabeth, the sculptor

Imagine yourself as Elizabeth, a talented sculptor who dreams of using her gift to inspire and uplift others through her captivating three-dimensional creations. Though you may face obstacles like self-doubt and criticism, can you see how your commitment to your goal – the transformative power of sculpture – propels you forward? Picture leaning on a network of fellow artists, mentors, and friends who understand your journey and encourage you during difficult times. How does their unwavering belief in your talent and the positive impact you can create strengthen your resolve? Through her commitment and resilience, Elizabeth continues to mould and shape clay, metal and stone into intricate sculptures that touch the hearts of many and spark a sense of wonder and introspection. Elizabeth's sculptures, with their flowing lines, intricate textures, and thought-provoking shapes, become tangible expressions of emotions and stories, inviting viewers to explore their own feelings and connect with the beauty and depth of the human experience.

Chloe, the advocate

Similarly, picture yourself as Chloe, an advocate for social justice and equality. Her gift lies in her ability to amplify marginalised voices and advocate for change. Have you felt frustration and resistance when pushing for change? Despite these setbacks, keep your commitment to a fair and inclusive society. Imagine the strength you draw from like-minded individuals. Surround yourself with those who share your vision and support your efforts. Each obstacle teaches you, doesn't it? And with each lesson learned, you refine your strategies and expand your network of allies. Like Chloe, inspire others to join the fight for social justice through your resilience and commitment.

Melody, the dancer

Now, step into the shoes of Melody, a professional dancer whose gift is to use movement to convey emotions and inspire others. Some call her a prophetic dancer because she hears the heart of God and uses her movements to bring about healing. Have you encountered physical challenges and moments of doubt? Melody has, and yet she stays committed to her craft, using her passion for dance to touch hearts and transform lives. She seeks mentors and coaches who understand the demands of her profession. Do you have mentors and supportive coaches in your life who provide guidance and encouragement? Their belief in your talent and their expertise help you develop resilience and strength. Through her commitment and resilience, Melody continues to pursue her passion for dance, captivating audiences with her performances and spreading joy through her art.

Remember to celebrate your successes, no matter how small they may seem. Each milestone achieved, every life touched, and every positive impact made is a cause for celebration. Do you acknowledge your growth, the lives you've influenced and the progress you've made? Recognising and appreciating your accomplishments fuels your motivation and builds the resilience needed to face future challenges.

Embrace every experience, whether perceived as positive or negative, as an opportunity for growth. Do you view setbacks as stepping stones rather than stumbling blocks? Each experience teaches valuable lessons and strengthens your resolve. Reflect, adapt, and use setbacks as fuel to drive your determination further.

During challenging times, have you surrounded yourself with a support system of friends, mentors, and fellow changemakers who uplift you? Their presence and belief in your abilities is a valuable reminder of your potential and can reignite your passion when it wavers. Together, you can overcome obstacles, celebrate successes, and navigate the twists and turns of your journey.

So, are you committed and resilient on your path of using your gift to serve others? Do you embrace challenges as opportunities for growth, celebrate your successes, and surround yourself with a supportive network? Always remember, setbacks do not define you but rather shape you into a stronger, more compassionate, and determined individual. Trust in your abilities, stay connected to your purpose, and let your unwavering commitment and resilience be the driving force that propels you forward.

ACTION STEPS FOR YOU:

Chapter 6 - Gift Unlocked: Make Your Mark on the World	
Align with your purpose	Embrace your gift as a means to achieving your purpose. Identify how your unique abilities can serve others and positively impact the world. Your gift is your instrument to create meaningful change.
Share your gift widely	Look for those who can benefit from your gift. Look for opportunities to share it, whether through volunteering, mentoring, or creative expression. The more you share, the more lives you can touch.
Persist with passion	Stay committed to your journey, fuelled by passion and resilience. Embrace growth as an ongoing process, and never be afraid to dream big. Your gift is a powerful tool for personal and global transformation.

Chapter 7

The Treasure Map: Hands-on Activities for Uncovering Your Gift

"Success is no accident. It is hard work, perseverance, learning, studying, sacrifice, and most of all, love of what you are doing or learning to do." - Pelé

Congratulations on beginning your exciting adventure of self-exploration, growth and empowerment. As you've journeyed through this book's pages, you've gained invaluable insights into your unique abilities and talents. Isn't it time now to take a step further and explore additional, engaging activities to reveal your hidden treasure?

Have you tried some of the suggested exercises yet? If not, don't worry. This chapter will give you the chance to dedicate some time to them. This is also an opportunity to reflect on your journey from when you first opened the book to where you stand now. Can you see the progress you've made?

Think of this chapter as your personal treasure map – your guide to the heart of your abilities, passions, and potential. Just like how a map uncovers hidden trails and secret destinations, these activities will light up the way to discovering your unique gift. Whether you're a student, a new mom, a career woman, a senior citizen or someone seeking clarity at life's crossroads, these exercises are tailored for you, regardless of your background or stage in life.

Every activity here is purposefully selected to ignite your curiosity, fuel your creativity, and unveil your hidden potential. Are you ready to dive into thought-provoking exercises, introspective journeys, and playful explorations leading to your unique gift?

This isn't about attaching a label or a title to your gift. Instead, it's about delving deep into your soul and revealing your authentic self. Can you see how uncovering your gift shapes your life and contributes to the world around you?

So, why not grab your journal and find a cosy corner? Let's start this treasure hunt together. Each activity is a stepping stone towards understanding yourself deeper, aligning with your passions, and connecting with your purpose. Let's dive in and explore the incredible world within you, releasing the potential that has been waiting to shine, shall we?

Remember, you are unique and empowered. Your self-discovery journey is a testament to your strength and courage. With every step you take, you're opening up new possibilities. Are you ready to unearth the treasure that is your gift with the tools provided in this chapter? Ready, set, let's begin!

1. Life Story Reflection: Connecting the Dots of Your Journey

Dare to delve into your life's journey and unravel the unique tapestry that is you? We all have a rich tapestry of life experiences, victories, challenges, and transformative moments that have shaped us into the amazing individuals we are today. This exercise is an invitation to explore the chapters of your life story and uncover the pivotal moments that have sculpted you into the exceptional person you are today. It's like decoding a treasure map that leads straight to your unique gift.

Find a calm and quiet space where you can reflect without any interruptions. Get a notebook or journal – or use the space provided in this book – and start writing those significant moments, milestones, and challenges that have left a lasting impression on your memory. Can you recall those times when you felt most alive, fulfilled, and authentically you? As you journey through your life's chapters, can you spot any recurring themes, passions, or interests that have endured over the years?

Take my experience for example. When I reflected on my life, I discovered that seeking counselling during a difficult period was a significant turning point. Not only did it assist me in navigating my struggles, but it ignited a passion within me – a deep-seated desire to help others. It was a gift that was waiting to be discovered. This intriguing world of counselling led me to pursue an educational journey, eventually earning a diploma in Counselling.

As I flipped through the pages of my life, I realised my newfound gift was ready to bloom. I established my own counselling practice, providing a sanctuary for individuals to share their struggles, find healing, and uncover their strengths. As I journeyed further, it became clear that I also had a natural inclination for coaching, which I incorporated into my services. Can you see how each step, each obstacle, each victory was a piece of the puzzle that led me to where I am now? The dots connected perfectly, revealing a gift I hadn't fully acknowledged until I took the time to ponder my journey.

This reflection exercise is designed to help you connect your experiences with your inherent tendencies. It's like assembling a puzzle, with each piece symbolising a part of your unique gift. As you unravel your life's story, can you see patterns beginning to surface? They are shedding light on your innate talents. This activity is not just a trip down memory lane, it's a bridge to self-discovery, guiding you towards understanding the threads that link your past, present, and the extraordinary potential that awaits you.

2. Mind Mapping Your Interests: Unveiling the Patterns of Your Passions

Have you ever thought of your mind as a vibrant canvas, brimming with the colours of your interests, hobbies, and passions? Mind mapping is a technique that allows you to visually capture the essence of what truly excites you. It's a tool that assists in untangling the complex web of your pursuits and revealing hidden aspects that might be your unique gift.

Ready to get started? All you need is a blank piece of paper or a digital mind mapping tool. Start at the centre by writing down a broad interest that resonates with you – could it be "creative expression" or "problem-solving"? Now, let your imagination take the reins. Branch out from your central theme with related interests, perhaps hobbies, activities or subjects that spark joy, curiosity, or a sense of fulfilment in you.

To give you an example, let's delve into my own mind map (see the image below). I made it simple so you can grasp the concept. At the very heart of it is my love for problem-solving. As I build out from there, the branches reveal my interest in communication/writing, which further leads to personal development, empowerment, and coaching. Another branch uncovers my fascination with psychology, intertwined with my desire to understand human behaviour and provide guidance. Each new branch provides fresh insights and connections, painting a vibrant picture of my interests that form the foundation of my unique gift.

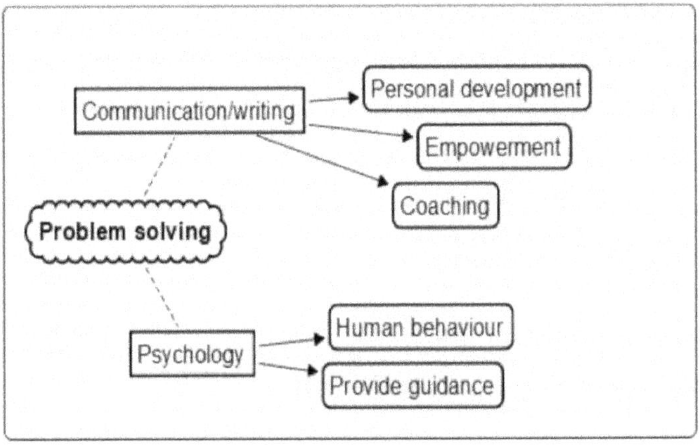

The magic of mind mapping is how it captures the multi-faceted nature of your passions. It allows you to see both the big picture and the intricate details, highlighting the connections and intersections between different interests. As you step back to admire your mind map, can you see any clusters forming? They could indicate the areas where your unique gifts truly shine. It's like looking at a constellation you've created – a visual demonstration of your potential waiting to be discovered.

So, why not try mind mapping your interests? It's an enjoyable and enlightening way to identify patterns and connections that could lead you to your unique gift. This journey of self-discovery invites you to explore the depths of your passions, revealing an array of possibilities. Through this activity, you'll gain a clearer understanding of what truly makes you come alive. Could this be the key to uncovering your real gift and paving the way for a transformative journey ahead?

3. Journalling Prompts: Crafting Your Gift's Narrative through Reflection

Think of your journal as your confidante, always ready to listen to your deepest thoughts, dreams, and aspirations. Have you ever pondered the power of journalling? It's a voyage of self-discovery, inviting you to dig deep into your soul to reveal your hidden treasures. Are you ready to embark on this exploration?

Why not set aside a specific time for journalling? Find a tranquil corner where you can commune with your thoughts, free from any distractions. Choose prompts that resonate with you, stirring you to reflect on your life, your interests, and your dreams. You could start with questions like: "What activities bring me joy?" or "When do I feel most engaged?" Gradually, you can venture into more profound questions.

Let me tell you about my personal journey with journalling. Reflecting on these prompts, I was transported back to my university years. I remembered leading group discussions, aiding my peers to unravel complex topics, and encouraging their participation. Can you think of a similar experience? That was when I felt a strong attraction towards mentoring, a hint of my talent that later developed into a deep passion for coaching and empowering others.

Do you see how journalling prompts can serve as a link between your thoughts and dreams? They nudge you to sift through your experiences, weaving together your passions and talents. As you delve into your responses, have you spotted any recurring themes, subtle inclinations, or even hidden wishes? Your journal is your canvas; it's where you paint your emerging talent, reflecting your unique self and your unexplored potential.

Here are five journalling prompts to help you unearth your inner gifts:

1. Reflect on Joyful Activities:

What activities make me feel joyous and fulfilled? When do I feel most vibrant and connected to my inner self? Explore moments that deeply resonate with your joy and satisfaction.

2. Recall Significant Life Moments:

Think about times in your life when you felt a strong passion. Can you remember a particular moment or experience that stirred something within you? Reflect on the circumstances and emotions of those times.

3. Identify Untapped Desires:

While journalling, look for any recurring themes, subtle inclinations, or desires that may be hiding in plain sight. Are there undiscovered passions or talents ready to be unveiled? Write about any hints or signs you uncover.

4. Explore Moments of Flow:

Think about times when you feel 'in the zone' – fully immersed in an activity. What are you doing during those moments, and how does it make you feel? Explore the aspects of those activities that resonate with your true self.

5. Connect Past Experiences with Present Passion:

Remember a time from your past, like my experience with leading group discussions in university. Have you had experiences that hinted at your gifts or passions? Connect those experiences to your current interests and consider how they may have shaped your unique narrative.

Why not incorporate journalling into your daily routine, making it a delightful ritual of introspection? Feel free to use these prompts as a starting point and allow your journalling journey to unfold naturally. Allow your thoughts to flow freely, without judgment or expectations. Let these journalling prompts lead you to the heart of your talent. With each line you write, you're illuminating your talents, dreams, and aspirations, crafting your unique story. Through journalling, you're empowering yourself to shape the narrative of your talent, one insightful entry at a time. Happy journalling!

4. Strengths and Weaknesses Analysis: Navigating the Seas of Self-Awareness

As you continue your voyage of self-discovery, consider me your compass, guiding you through the vast seas of self-awareness. Your first task is to identify your strengths and weaknesses, two significant factors that map out your potential.

You might remember we've touched upon this topic before. However, as you've journeyed this far into self-discovery, revisiting this concept is crucial to your growth. Were you a little shy when you first tried to identify your strengths and acknowledge your weaknesses? There's no need for that now. This is your chance to be honest with yourself and pinpoint these defining factors with confidence.

So, where do we begin? Let's start by celebrating your strengths, those distinctive qualities that make you stand out. Remember those moments when you felt a surge of confidence and competence. Were you able to solve complex problems with ease, engage in meaningful conversations, or perhaps create stunning works of art without breaking a sweat? It's time to acknowledge these talents. Think of it as opening a treasure chest, each gem inside representing a unique strength.

But remember, our journey doesn't end with strengths. We must also navigate the shores of our weaknesses. Do you view them as stumbling blocks? It's time to see them as stepping stones on the path to growth. Can you recall a time when you faced challenges or setbacks? Maybe you found public speaking terrifying, or perhaps time management was a struggle? These instances aren't failures, they're perfect opportunities to identify areas for improvement and broaden your skills.

Take my personal journey, for example. During a career transition, I discovered that my organisational and problem-solving skills were strong anchors. Yet, I also found I was weak in public speaking. Instead of being discouraged, I took it as a chance to improve my communication skills through workshops and constant practice.

Remember, your strengths are the torch lighting your path and your weaknesses, the compass guiding your growth. Embrace both with open arms, they're equally important on your journey. By understanding where you shine and where you need to polish, you’re essentially building a roadmap that enables you to navigate the oceans of self-awareness and set a course towards discovering your unique gift. Your strengths are the sails that propel you forward, and your weaknesses, the winds that fill them, pushing you towards the treasure of your untapped potential.

5. Hobby Analysis: Unveiling Your Joyful Pursuits

Imagine your life as a canvas, with each hobby and creative indulgence acting as a unique brushstroke, painting a picture of your soul. It's the brushstroke that reveals a bit of the masterpiece that is you. Indulging in activities that spark joy and fulfilment is essentially a way of self-expression, a hint to your exclusive gift.

Now, take a moment to think about your hobbies, those activities that truly bring you joy. Feel the spark that ignites each time you engage in those pursuits that set your spirit ablaze. Do you find fulfilment in penning down words into poetry? Perhaps it's the quiet serenity of gardening or the creative burst of cooking a new recipe. Maybe it's the harmony of playing a musical instrument, the freedom of paint meeting canvas. Can you recall those moments where you were so engrossed in what you were doing that time seemed to dissolve? Those are the moments when you're in sync with your authentic self, tapping into your innate talents and passions.

Take Aurélie's story, for instance. She discovered her love for writing during quiet moments when she filled pages with her thoughts. It was more than just a hobby; through journalling, she found comfort and a sense of empowerment. Eventually, Aurélie turned this hobby into a career, using words to inspire and connect with others. It was through writing that she found her unique gift – communication and storytelling. Can you relate to this?

Let me share my own experience with you. I found one of my gifts in an unexpected place – a hobby. After becoming a mother at an age when most women are watching their children grow up, I faced many challenges. Are you familiar with my story? I decided to share my journey through a YouTube channel, hoping to support other mothers facing similar situations. What began as a simple hobby evolved into something more – a platform where I could connect with and inspire others. Today, I have a thriving community of over 7,000 subscribers, providing support and empowerment to new mothers over 40.

Your hobbies are not just pastimes; they're a roadmap to your purpose. Have you ever thought about exploring them further? Pay attention to the activities that fill you with joy and excitement. They are your compass, guiding you towards your unique gifts. Remember, just like every brushstroke contributes to a masterpiece, every hobby you engage in reveals a part of you and the intricate artwork that is your life.

6. Feedback Analysis: Discovering Your Impact Through Others' Eyes

Have you ever pondered the power of feedback? Picture a mirror that shows you more than just your physical reflection, one that peers deep into your soul and potential. Think of feedback as that mirror, providing you with invaluable insights that you may not discover alone. This is the power of feedback, a tool that offers you a chance to see yourself through the eyes of those who know you best. They can shed light on your talents and strengths in ways that might surprise you.

Feedback is a priceless gift, a window into how you impact others' lives. When was the last time you actively sought feedback from your friends, family, or mentors? These people understand you, your journey and passions, and can provide insights into your unique qualities. Engage them in meaningful conversations. What do they see as your strengths and potential? What sets you apart?

Allow me to share another personal story. When I asked for feedback, I was pleasantly surprised to learn that my closest friends valued my listening skills and guidance – qualities I hadn't fully acknowledged. Their words opened my eyes to the fact that my empathetic and compassionate nature had a profound effect on those around me. Can you guess what happened next? This revelation motivated me to pursue a career in counselling, leading me to complete a counselling diploma and establish my own practice. Their input transformed a corner of my heart into a wellspring of purpose and empowerment.

Now, take Gloria's story, for instance. She's a fervent advocate for sustainability. When she discussed her passion with her circle, they highlighted her unique ability to inspire and educate others about eco-friendly practices. This feedback encouraged Gloria to use her exceptional communication skills to effect positive change. She went on to start workshops that educate communities about sustainable living. Can you see how by embracing feedback, Gloria realised her potential and channelled it into making a difference?

Feedback is like a mirror reflecting your unique brilliance. It's a tool that helps you see aspects of yourself that might be obscured by self-doubt or modesty. Are you ready to open yourself to the insights of those who care about you? By welcoming feedback, you gather precious pieces of the puzzle that forms your unique gift.

Remember, feedback is a treasure, providing a glimpse into how you influence those around you. As you continue your journey of self-discovery, are you ready to embrace the wisdom of others' perspectives? Can you let their words guide you towards empowerment and impact? Your transformation may well depend on these.

7. Dream Analysis: Navigating the Terrain of Your Aspirations

Have you ever tried to delve into your dreams to uncover your deepest aspirations? Your dreams are more than just night-time narratives; they are signposts to your unique gifts and desires. Think about the recurring themes in your dreams. Do you often find yourself leading others? Or perhaps you are immersed in an artistic endeavour that fills you with joy? Behind these scenarios lie a window to your passions and talents, offering a glimpse of the change you could bring about. What kind of transformation do you envision bringing about?

Take the case of Eunice. She had dreams where she was at the heart of a busy beauty salon, delivering personalised skincare treatments and makeup services. This recurring dream revealed Eunice's deep-seated desire to turn her passion for beauty therapy into a successful business.

Inspired by her dream revelations, Eunice took action. She enrolled in entrepreneurship courses and meticulously planned every aspect of her new venture. Despite facing challenges, her determination never wavered, and she eventually launched her beauty salon. Eunice's dream not only fulfilled her own aspirations but also created a positive impact on her clients' lives. Doesn't Eunice's journey inspire you to pursue your dreams with unwavering determination?

Now, let's talk about Sabine. She dreamed of a serene oasis filled with lush gardens. These dreams unveiled Sabine's true calling and her innate ability to nurture and promote growth. Through analysing her dreams, she recognised her affinity for plants was more than just a hobby – it was a reflection of her natural talent.

Motivated by her dreams, Sabine decided to establish a community garden – a place for people to come together, learn, and thrive. She poured her heart and soul into this project, and her garden soon became a symbol of growth and renewal, a testament to the transformative power of nature and community. Sabine's story is a perfect example of how our dreams can guide us towards creating something truly extraordinary.

Your dreams are whispering your passions and talents to you. Are you ready to listen to them, just like Eunice and Sabine did? Remember, when you heed their call, you have the potential to leave a legacy of growth, beauty, and connection that will endure for generations to come. So, are you ready to navigate the terrain of your dreams and turn them into reality?

You too can explore your dreams. Start by keeping a dream journal. Note down the vibrant settings, characters, and emotions that visit you in your sleep. Over time, patterns may surface, pointing you towards activities and pursuits that resonate with your true self. Let your dreams guide you on your journey to self-discovery. They have the potential to reveal your unique gift and set you on a path that mirrors your deepest desires.

Your dreams are the doorway to your aspirations. And your aspirations are not just wishful thinking; they are subtle hints of your gift, encouraging you to discover and harness your true potential. They chart a course to your passions and the impact you wish to make. By heeding the recurring themes in your day and night dreams, you can unearth your unique gift. Welcome the insights your dreams provide and let them steer you towards a life of purpose, fulfilment, and transformation.

8. Meditation and Visualisation Techniques: Nurturing the Seeds of Your Gift

Have you ever considered creating a peaceful garden within your mind? A sanctuary from the outside noise, where you can truly hear your inner voice? Techniques such as meditation and visualisation offer a powerful way to (re)focus your mind, increase wellness and reach your goals. Here, you'll find the roots of your talents and passions.

Let's start with meditation, which is really about expanding your sense of awareness. It’s like having a new perspective on life; seeing your thoughts and feelings from a distance, without judging them. It’s a way to know yourself better. I, for instance, do this by focusing my mind on God or Bible verses. It’s certainly not about emptying your mind.

This practice encourages stillness and presence. Can you find a quiet space, a refuge from the outside world's noise and distractions? It doesn’t mean sitting down for hours, it just means that you take time to reflect on your day or on God's Word and learn how to apply it to your life.

Now, try focusing on your breathing as an example. Sit comfortably. Let your spine stretch out and release the tension from your shoulders. Close your eyes gently and turn your attention to your breathing.

As you inhale, can you feel the cool air entering your nostrils? Notice how your chest and abdomen expand as your lungs fill with air. On the exhale, can you feel the warm breath leaving your body? Let each breath anchor you in this present moment, grounding you in the here and now.

As you maintain focus on your breath, you might notice your mind's chatter starting to fade away. Thoughts may still arise, but instead of getting caught up in them, can you simply acknowledge their presence and then gently return your focus to your breath? With each inhale and exhale, allow yourself to sink deeper into relaxation and inner stillness.

During meditation, you may encounter vivid images, thoughts, and emotions bubbling up from your subconscious. These are fragments of your authentic self, ready to be acknowledged and embraced. Can you tune into the sensations arising in your body, the memories surfacing from your mind's recesses, and the emotions stirring within you?

These experiences provide clues to your natural inclinations and deepest desires. Maybe you visualise scenes from your past that bring joy or nostalgia. Or you might unearth buried emotions that have been waiting for recognition and processing. Whatever surfaces during meditation, trust that it carries significance and wisdom for your self-discovery journey.

By maintaining a regular meditation practice, you create room for your inner wisdom to surface and guide you. Each moment of stillness and presence deepens your connection to yourself, providing insight into your true nature. Are you ready to use meditation as a potent tool to uncover hidden aspects of yourself and align with your life's authentic purpose?

I would like to share my personal experience with the transformative power of meditation and visualisation practices. Over the last half decade, I have been deeply engaged in understanding and practicing meditation and visualisation, gaining insights and inspirations that have significantly influenced my life's journey.

To me, meditation is not merely a routine, but a revered ritual of self-exploration and inner discovery. Despite my hectic schedule as a mother, every day, I manage to find a serene corner within my home to escape the daily grind and immerse myself in profound tranquillity. I create an environment free from interruptions, with my phone set to silent, the television switched off, and devoid of any distracting noise. When my young child is at daycare, spending time with his father, or blissfully asleep, I take a moment to sit comfortably, shut my eyes, and focus my attention on the calming rhythm of my breathing. This solitary moment allows me to surrender to the present, welcoming the serenity that meditation imparts.

As I inhale and exhale, I feel the day's stress dissolve, replaced by a deep calm and peace. In this state of internal quiet, I foster an environment where my inner wisdom can grow and reveal itself. Thoughts may come and go, but I gently let them drift away, refocusing my attention on my steady breath.

Meditation has helped me nurture a profound connection with myself and the world around me. I've uncovered hidden depths of inner strength and resilience, accessing a source of bravery and lucidity I was previously unaware of. Each moment of tranquillity brings me a step closer to understanding my true self and the journey I am destined to embark on.

However, the most transformative element of my journey has been my exploration of visualisation. It is about letting your mind paint a picture of what you want or where you want to be. It's like a mental movie of something you want to happen. It's a powerful tool that people use when they're meditating, trying to stay in the moment, or setting big goals. It's a way of seeing success before it happens, which helps make it a reality.

Annually, I commit to crafting a vision board – a form of visualisation. It's a vibrant montage of pictures, quotes, and symbols that encapsulate my deepest aspirations and dreams. One consistent dream among the diverse visions on my board is to author an inspirational book that resonates with others.

Looking at my vision board fills me with an invigorating surge of energy and creativity. I can almost visualise the words pouring out of me onto an empty page, crafting a narrative of hope and healing for those who need it the most. Through visualisation, I've given life to this dream, fostering it with deliberate intention until it materialised into reality.

Today, as I begin writing, I am overwhelmed by a deep sense of gratitude and accomplishment. What once seemed an unattainable dream has now come to fruition, mirroring my deepest yearnings. Through the practices of meditation and visualisation, I've opened the gateway to limitless possibilities, enabling my most authentic self to radiate and enlighten the world with its luminosity.

My personal journey stands as evidence of the transformative potential of these practices. Meditation has allowed me to find peace in turmoil and clarity amidst ambiguity. Visualisation has breathed existence into my dreams, allowing them to soar on the wings of intention and belief. Throughout this journey, I've unearthed the immense potential that resides within us all, poised to be stirred and realised.

Can you visualise yourself participating in activities that bring you joy, fulfilment, and purpose? How do you feel? Excitement, contentment, passion?

Let's take the example of Lisa. She discovered her innate talent for public speaking through this very method – the simple act of visualising it. Can you imagine closing your eyes and seeing yourself confidently addressing a captivated audience, feeling a surge of energy and purpose? That's exactly what Lisa did.

Picture this: Lisa standing tall on a stage, her voice resonating with conviction, delivering a powerful message that touches the hearts of her listeners. Can you hear the applause? Can you sense the admiration of the audience? This is what fuelled Lisa's passion, reinforced her belief in her ability and became a driving force in her life. Could this be the same for you?

Motivated by the clarity and confidence from her visualisations, Lisa committed to public speaking as her way of sharing her message with the world. Despite initial doubts or fears, she was determined to step into the spotlight. Would you also be willing to face your fears in order to inspire change?

As Lisa began her public speaking journey, she encountered challenges. There were moments of doubt and uncertainty, yet she refused to let these hinder her progress. Instead, she turned to visualisation as her strength and guidance. Could visualisation also serve as your source of strength in times of uncertainty?

With each public speaking engagement, Lisa sharpened her skills and refined her message. She drew upon the confidence and clarity she had cultivated through visualisation. As she shared her insights and experiences, she witnessed the transformative power of her words. Could you also inspire others with your authentic voice?

Through visualisation, Lisa not only discovered her gift for public speaking but also unleashed her full potential as a catalyst for change. Isn't it empowering to imagine that you, too, could unlock your hidden talents, overcome obstacles, and create a reality aligned with your deepest aspirations by harnessing the power of visualisation? Lisa's journey serves as a powerful reminder of the profound impact visualisation can have on our lives. So, what's stopping you from visualising your own success?

Meditation and visualisation are powerful tools for self-discovery. They help you connect with your hidden talents and passions. Can you imagine the potential you could unlock by incorporating these practices into your daily routine? Embrace these techniques and watch the seeds of your gift grow into reality.

9. Online Quizzes and Assessments: Unveiling Your Hidden Strengths

If you're feeling a bit stuck or uncertain about your unique gifts and talents, don't worry. In today's digital age, a wealth of resources is at your fingertips. In fact, there's a modern and fun way to get some valuable insights. Let's talk about online quizzes and assessments! Those little questionnaires that can help you uncover your strengths, interests, and even point you in the direction of your purpose.

Although we explored the notion of quizzes and self-assessments earlier in the book – in Chapter 2 – I feel it is important to delve deeper into this topic.

So, picture this: you're relaxing with your favourite cup of tea, scrolling through the web, and you stumble upon a personality quiz or a strengths assessment. These quizzes are like treasure maps for your soul – they guide you through a series of questions that reveal different facets of your personality, preferences, and potential. Think of it as a cool virtual journey that shines a light on the amazing qualities that make you, well, you!

Let me get personal for a moment. I remember a time when I was on the hunt for some self-discovery magic. I came across an online quiz that promised insights into my strengths and personality – something I mentioned in Chapter 2 of the book, as you may recall. I was intrigued, so I gave it a try. The result? It described me as an "Insightful Contributor" – someone who's all about making a positive impact, organising things, and helping others grow. It felt like a personalised high-five from the universe!

But here's the thing: online quizzes are like a compass, not a GPS. They provide you with hints and clues about your strengths, but they're not the ultimate guide. Take me, for instance. The quiz gave me a glimpse of my strengths, but it was the weaving together of these results with my life experiences that truly helped me understand myself better.

And you know what's great? These quizzes give you words to describe your strengths. Suddenly, you're armed with the perfect way to tell the world about what makes you awesome. It's like having a secret decoder ring for unlocking your unique abilities!

But wait, there's more. These quizzes can sometimes lead you to paths you never thought of before. Remember, they're like friendly nudges, not destiny makers. They offer suggestions, but the real magic happens when you mix their insights with your own feelings and thoughts.

So, go ahead and dive into the world of online quizzes and assessments. It's like a virtual treasure hunt for your talents. And remember, this is just one piece of the puzzle. Blend the knowledge from these quizzes with your own reflections, dreams, and experiences. That's how you craft a beautiful tapestry of your strengths and purpose. So, grab that cup of tea and start exploring – you're on the path to discovering the amazing gift that is YOU!

At the very start of this book, I made available a quiz designed to give you insights into your strengths and passions, paving the way for your journey of using your gift to make a positive impact on the world. This quiz is called **"How Empowered Are You?"**. This section will be used to reflect on the answers you provided and what the outcome you received means for you.

With that said, here is the full list of scores and corresponding types of empowerment. There are four states of empowerment. According to the result you received, the extended description of your state of empowerment is aimed at inspiring you on your journey of transformation:

State of Empowerment #1: **Sparkling Radiance**

Result: You carry within yourself an immense sense of empowerment that illuminates your being. Your special talent is outstanding and has the capability to bring about transformative changes in people's lives.

Who It's For: This is for those who have accepted their unique gift and are using it to bring about a substantial positive shift in others' lives. They emanate self-assuredness and genuineness in their empowerment journey.

Significance: Your steadfast devotion to constant personal growth and the courage to face challenges has allowed your special talent to reach its peak potential. Your glowing aura serves as an inspiration and source of upliftment for those around you.

Details: Your empowering aura and real passion for your special talent magnetise people towards you. You are open to learning and enhancing your skills, which further augments your influence.

Next Steps: Continue to cultivate your unique talent and use it as a catalyst for positive change. Keep inspiring and empowering others through your deeds. Your luminous empowerment has the potential to cause a chain reaction of positive transformations in many people's lives.

State of Empowerment #2: **Flourishing Strength**

Result: Your empowerment is on the rise, providing you with the fortitude to accept your unique talent and use it to make a positive difference.

Who It's For: Individuals who are starting to identify and utilise their unique power and are gathering the courage to share it with the world.

Significance: You hold the capability to face and overcome obstacles while continuing your path towards empowerment. Your determination is what sparks your will to influence others positively.

Details: Even though you're still in the development phase, your unique talent holds immense promise, and your actions exhibit a fresh sense of ambition and guidance.

Next Steps: Persistently nurture your talent and always look for ways to broaden your knowledge and skills. With unwavering determination and ongoing development, you will unlock even more potential to bring about enduring transformation.

State of Empowerment #3: **Blossoming Confidence**

Result: Your sense of empowerment is flourishing, and your unique talent has the potential to motivate and inspire.

Who It's For: Those who are starting to appreciate the worth of their talent and are becoming more comfortable in showcasing it.

Significance: Your growing self-confidence and the positive effects of your talent on others are contributing to a flourishing sense of empowerment.

Details: You are moving beyond your comfort zone and interacting with others, revealing your talent to the world.

Next Steps: Face challenges head-on and have faith in your abilities. As your assurance strengthens, the influence of your talent will likewise grow. Continue to nurture your potential, and your talent will persistently bloom and have a positive impact on many lives.

State of Empowerment #4: **Rising Potential**

Result: Your capacity for empowerment is expanding, and your unique talent is brimming with immense promise.

Who It's For: This is for those who are beginning to understand the strength of their abilities and are keen to explore its potential.

Significance: Your dedication to ongoing development and education is driving you onwards, unleashing the vast promise of your talent.

Details: You exhibit a readiness to confront new hurdles and welcome the path of self-realisation and empowerment.

Next Steps: Immerse yourself in the path of perpetual advancement. As you cultivate and polish your talent, its reach will amplify, impacting numerous lives. Continue to refine your abilities, and your escalating potential will guide you in making a significant and enduring difference in the world.

If at any point you feel the need for guidance and support on your life-changing journey towards elevated empowerment, contemplate engaging with a coach or a mentor. They can provide tailored strategies and motivation to help you unlock your maximum potential and surmount any challenges that might arise. Welcome the assistance at your disposal and witness your confidence prosper, making a significant difference in the world.

So, which state of empowerment are you in? Are you surprised by your result?

Online quizzes and assessments are like keys that unlock the doors to your potential. Embrace them as opportunities to uncover new facets of yourself and reaffirm existing strengths. Approach these tools with an open heart and a curious mind, allowing them to illuminate the path ahead. As you navigate the digital landscape of self-discovery, remember that every quiz taken, every insight gained, contributes to the unfolding story of your unique gift.

My Final Words

The Journey Continues

Dear Reader,

As we approach the final pages of this transformative book, I want to take a moment to thank you. Can you feel it? That sense of excitement and anticipation? Your journey of self-discovery is only just beginning, and your natural gifts are like a beacon shining in the darkness. Do you believe that your gift has the potential to bring you joy and fulfilment, while also enriching the lives of those around you?

And let's not forget, your gift isn't something to be kept hidden or underestimated. It's something to be treasured, nurtured, and developed. Embrace it and let it guide you towards a life of purpose and meaning. With every step you take into the depths of your gift, you'll uncover talents and abilities that will leave you in awe of what you're capable of.

Life, of course, will throw obstacles in your path. But isn't it true that these obstacles are opportunities in disguise? They test our resolve, build our resilience, and teach us invaluable lessons about ourselves. I encourage you to embrace these challenges with courage and determination. Will you let the fire within you burn brightly, igniting your passion and propelling you forward?

Remember, the gift you're uncovering isn't only for your own benefit. It's for the world to share in. Just imagine using your gift to bring hope, joy, and relief to others. See how transformative it is to serve others. By doing so, you'll discover a sense of purpose and fulfilment that exceeds all expectations.

And don't forget, your gift isn't limited to a singular expression. It's like a multifaceted gem, reflecting different aspects of who you are. Take time to explore the vast array of possibilities that lie before you. Perhaps you can inspire with your words, paint emotions on a canvas, or heal with your compassionate touch. The choices are limitless.

As you continue on this remarkable journey, don't hesitate to seek guidance and support. Have you thought about reaching out to like-minded individuals who understand the power of your gift? What about seeking a coach, or investing in courses and workshops to further develop your skills? Remember, investing in yourself is the most valuable investment you can make.

As we wrap up, I want you to understand this fundamental truth – your inherent talent is a truly powerful tool. Let it guide you, leading you to a life enriched with purpose and fulfilment. The world awaits the unique impact you're destined to make, and I am positive that your journey of self-discovery will continue to unfold in remarkable ways.

But remember, this isn't the end, it's just the beginning. There are numerous more adventures to pursue, wisdom to gain, and obstacles to overcome. I urge you to persevere in your search for knowledge, expanding your horizons, and embracing new challenges. Remember, what you carry is an infinite source of potential that grows and flourishes the more you tap into it.

You have the power to shape your future and create a legacy that will inspire future generations. I believe in you and I pledge to stand with you, supporting you at every turn. Together, let's unveil and maximise your gift's full potential to create a lasting impact on the world.

So, as you flip the last pages of this book, realise that it doesn't mark the end, but a magnificent new beginning. Let this be the ignition that propels you towards a future filled with purpose, enthusiasm, and fulfilment. Explore the opportunities that await you, and rest assured that I am here, ready to guide you on this transformative journey.

I extend my heartfelt thanks for staying the course. As you acknowledge and nurture your talent, I wish you nothing but the best as you embrace your greatness and craft a life that is truly EXTRA-ordinary. Treasure your journey, stay resolute, and let your gift shine brightly as you bring about a positive change in your life and those of others. Remember, you are gifted and empowered. Now go out there and illuminate the world with your brilliance!

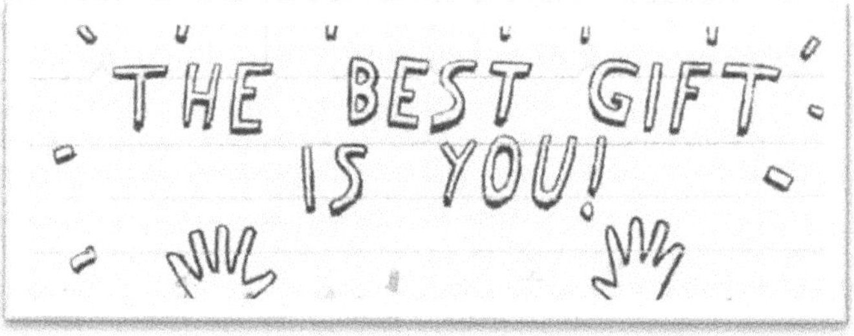

WHAT IS YOUR SPECIAL GIFT?

TAKE THE 2ND QUIZ BELOW:

"WHAT IS YOUR SPECIAL GIFT?"

You can access the quiz via the QR code above or please go to: https://mindfulteabreak.involve.me/what-is-your-special-gift

Your answers will provide valuable insights into your unique gift and the potential impact you can create in the world! Embark on a transformative journey of using your gift to serve others.

If you would like to discuss your results, feel free to book a call with me at: hello@caroledmonteiro.com

Results from the "What's Your Special Gift" quiz:

#1 - Type of special gift: Creative Expressions

Outcome: You possess the gift of Creative Expressions, where you find joy and fulfilment by expressing yourself through arts, crafts, or any other creative medium. Your unique talent lies in bringing beauty and inspiration to life through your imaginative mind and artistic endeavors. Whether it's painting vibrant canvases, crafting heartfelt poetry, composing soul-stirring melodies, or engaging in any other creative pursuit, your creations have the power to touch people's hearts, evoke deep emotions, and leave a lasting impact on those who experience them.

Who it's for: Creative individuals who have a passion for expressing themselves through various forms of art. Your creativity and unique perspective make you a true visionary. Your gift of Creative Expressions allows you to connect with others on a profound level, as you believe in the transformative power of creativity to bring joy and inspiration to people's lives. In short, you are a Creative Visionary!

Significance: Your gift is a reflection of your inner world, where you possess the ability to convey emotions, thoughts, and ideas in ways that words often fail to capture. Your unique perspective and keen eye for beauty enable your creations to stand out and resonate with others.

Specifics: Your artistic talents are not merely a hobby but a powerful tool for transforming lives. Through your creative expressions and innovative thinking, you have the potential to brighten someone's day, provide comfort in times of sorrow, or inspire them to pursue their own artistic passions. Your art becomes a means of communication that transcends language barriers, reaching deep into the souls of those who experience it.

Next steps: Embrace your gift of Creative Expressions and use it to create meaningful connections with others. Share your art through public exhibitions, online platforms, or intimate gatherings to touch the hearts of those who need it most. Your ability to inspire and uplift others through your art is a gift that can bring joy and healing to the world.

#2 - Type of special gift: Empathetic Support

Outcome: Your gift is Empathetic Support, where you have the ability to offer comfort, understanding, and encouragement to those in need. Your compassionate nature and genuine concern for others make you a valuable pillar of strength in their lives. Your presence provides solace and assurance, helping others navigate through challenging times.

Who it's for: Empathetic and caring individuals who naturally gravitate towards helping others. You are a reliable and understanding friend, always ready to lend a listening ear and a comforting shoulder to lean on. In short, you are an Empathetic Helper!

Significance: Your gift of Empathetic Support comes from your deep sense of compassion and your willingness to be there for others without judgment. You have an innate ability to understand and uplift the spirits of those around you, making them feel valued and cared for.

Specifics: People seek you out when they need someone to talk to, knowing that you genuinely care about their well-being. Your capacity to offer encouragement and emotional support is a gift that can create a safe space for healing and growth in the lives of those you touch. Your empathetic nature allows you to connect with others on a profound level, making them feel understood and accepted.

Next steps: Embrace your gift of Empathetic Support and continue being a source of comfort and encouragement for those around you. Consider volunteering or working in fields that allow you to channel your gift into helping others, such as counselling, caregiving, or support group facilitation. Your ability to uplift and empower others is a powerful force for positive change in the world.

#3 - Type of special gift: Analytical Problem-Solving

Outcome: Your gift is being an Analytical Problem-Solver. You have a keen ability to dissect complex issues, analyse data, and provide practical solutions that positively impact the lives of others. Your analytical thinking and strategic approach make you a valuable asset in any situation, helping you navigate challenges with foresight and ingenuity.

Who it's for: Analytical and logical thinkers who enjoy tackling challenges head-on and finding innovative solutions. You thrive in environments that require critical thinking and problem-solving skills. In short, you are an Analytical Strategist!

Significance: Your gift of being an Analytical Problem-Solver is a result of your sharp intellect and dedication to understanding the root causes of issues. You approach problems with a clear and methodical mindset, allowing you to break them down into manageable pieces and find effective solutions.

Specifics: Your strategic prowess enables you to see patterns, make connections, and identify opportunities that others might miss. Whether it's in professional settings, personal relationships, or community projects, your gift of problem-solving can lead to positive outcomes and greater efficiency. You possess the ability to think critically and objectively, making well-informed decisions that positively impact individuals and organisations alike.

Next steps: Embrace your gift of being an Analytical Problem-Solver and apply it to areas where your expertise can make a significant impact. Consider careers in fields like business analysis, data science, research, project management, or consulting, where your abilities can shine. Your gift has the potential to solve complex issues and contribute to a better world for everyone.

#4 - Type of special gift: Inspirational Motivation

Outcome: You possess the gift of Inspirational Motivation. Your words and actions have the power to uplift and empower those around you, igniting a fire of determination and belief in themselves. Your ability to lead and inspire makes you a catalyst for positive change.

Who it's for: Inspirational individuals who naturally motivate others through their words, actions, or leadership. You have a gift for instilling confidence and courage in those you interact with. In short, you are an Inspirational Motivator!

Significance: Your gift of being an Inspirational Motivator comes from your natural charisma, optimism, and passion for uplifting others. Your genuine belief in people's potential and ability to overcome challenges makes them feel encouraged and empowered.

Specifics: Your inspirational words can touch the hearts of many, instilling hope and courage even in the face of adversity. Whether you are speaking in public, mentoring, or simply being a role model, your gift has a profound impact on the lives of others. Your positive energy and unwavering support inspire those around you to reach for their dreams and strive for greatness.

Next steps: Embrace your gift of being an Inspirational Motivator and use it to empower others to pursue their dreams and make a positive impact. Consider becoming a motivational speaker, a life coach, a mentor, a team leader, or a community organiser. Your ability to inspire others is a gift that can ignite a spark of greatness in those around you.

Share your wisdom and encouragement with the world, and watch as you bring out the best in others, unlocking their full potential for a brighter future.

#5 - Type of special gift: The Resilient Champion

Outcome: Your gift lies in your unwavering resilience and ability to bounce back from setbacks. You see challenges as stepping-stones to personal growth and inspire others to do the same. Your extraordinary ability to turn challenges into opportunities for growth and inspire others along the way is a true gift.

Who it's for: Resilient individuals who view setbacks as opportunities for growth and believe in the power of perseverance. Your gift as The Resilient Champion makes you a beacon of strength and hope for those around you. In short, you are an Inspirational Resilient!

Significance: Your gift of resilience is a product of your unwavering spirit and determination to overcome obstacles. Instead of being defeated by adversity, you use it as fuel to thrive and motivate others to do the same.

Specifics: Your remarkable ability to bounce back from setbacks serves as a powerful example to others, showing them that they too can rise above challenges and emerge stronger. Your journey of personal growth and triumph over adversity becomes a source of inspiration and encouragement for those who face difficult times.

Next steps: Embrace your gift as The Resilient Champion and continue to inspire others with your resilience. Share your experiences and life lessons with those who need a guiding light in their darkest moments. Consider becoming a social worker, a resilience coach, an advocate for mental health, a training and development specialist, or a mentor for individuals seeking strength during tough times. Your gift has the potential to ignite a spark of hope in the hearts of many and lead them towards their own path of triumph and empowerment.

COACHING SESSION INVITATION

I hope that you have enjoyed reading my book.

This was truly a labour of love, and it was an honour to help you in your journey to harness your unique gifts and to purposely leave a legacy.

If you feel like you need more clarity on your quiz results, need additional support or guidance on your journey of empowerment, and would like to discuss getting help, then I would love to talk with you.

In celebration of my first book, I would like to extend a personal invitation to you for a complimentary coaching session.

This is not a sales call – my only intention is to find out more about you and your goals to see if and how I can help you.

Due to time constraints, the call will be limited to twenty minutes – nonetheless worth both our time.

Are you ready to get started?

Contact me directly at hello@caroledmonteiro.com to book your complimentary coaching session today and use the word “GIFTED” as a reference.

CONTACT INFORMATION

Carole can be reached at:
hello@caroledmonteiro.com

Author website:
https://www.caroledmonteiro.com

Like Carole's author page on Goodreads:
https://www.goodreads.com/book/show/213672977-gifted-and-empowered

Carole's Linktree:
https://linktr.ee/caroledmonteiro

Follow Carole on Instagram: @caroledmonteiro

Follow Carole on LinkedIn:
https://www.linkedin.com/in/carole-d-monteiro-a4942b258

Follow Carole on her French-speaking YouTube channel dedicated to new moms: @maman-etc

Carole's Coaching services:
https://www.MindfulTeaBreak.com

FEEDBACK REQUEST

Did you enjoy this book?

Your feedback helps me provide the best quality books and helps other readers like you discover great books.

It would mean the world to me if you took 2 minutes to **share your thoughts about this book as a review**. You can leave a review on the retailer of your choice and/or send me an email with your honest feedback:

https://mybook.to/GiftedAndEmpowered

Milton Keynes UK
Ingram Content Group UK Ltd.
UKHW022055260924
448786UK00012B/566